MAN

&

METAPHYSICS

A Search For The Real Man

Donald H. Yott

SAMUEL WEISER NEW YORK

Published in 1980 by
Samuel Weiser Inc.
740 Broadway
New York, N.Y. 10003

ISBN-0-87728-488-1

Printed in the U.S.A. by
Noble Offset Printers, Inc.
New York, N.Y. 10003

Dedicated to
Alice D. Fowler and John Hay — my teachers
and early mentors in this field of study
and
Joel R. Walder
for recent encouragement and inspiration

Foreword

When the author requested of us to read the manuscript for this volume and to write the Forward, we thought it odd that he would select us — one a persistent challenger (on a religious basis) of his occult philosophy and the other an open-minded skeptic.

In the decade that we've known Donald Yott, we have seen the velocity of change in our environment outstrip man's ability to cope with change.

Young people and young adults, in almost every country, now outnumber their elders. They question — and mock — the values imposed by the older generations.

Minorities, recently aware of their unrealized potentials, demand even more acceleration in the pace of change.

Technologies, while providing amazing material abundance, have also opened the flood gates on a flow of effluvia that the other parts of nature cannot handle.

Organized religions, frequently the last to catch up to changing needs, are beset by chaotic pressures from within and without that appear to leave them adrift and rudderless.

Donald Yott has put together some of his lectures in this book in an attempt to express that which is inexpressable. If read as an introductory course of instruction, it can shed some different perspectives on the changes that appear to be making shambles out of our established cultures.

It suggests some ways that individuals might deal with change. And, indeed, it might start a reader on the way to identifying the very nature of change itself.

If read as a series of essays, there are many points of commonality with orthodox religious thought, but he is not touting religion.

There are admonitions for those who would impose either anarchy or new order that SELF-government is a prerequisite to living and developing in any system in nature, political, religious or cultural.

He suggests some steps for individuals to take to get with the higher laws of nature. None of them are leaps. Thay are small, difficult steps.

It would be unfair not to include some cautions in this age of instant food, fast-acting pills, and programmed palliatives.

This book offers no new system of thinking or prepared values to live by. Reading it is challenging work. Understanding it is more work.

It is not unlike looking toward a frosted window. You know there is some kind of light on the other side of the window but until it is opened, you cannot really define the source or the quality of the light. It could be warming, gentle, and invigorating as a spring sun; it could be blinding and overpowering.

So this book cracks the window a little. As you look through the opening, squint a little with your mind. Let your outlook broaden slowly and your perceptions deepen solidly and gradually.

This is especially important as the last two chapters are approached. The author's discussion of meditation might be an easy one into which to jump and just as easy to drown in. There are probably as many methods of meditation as there are meditators. You cannot meditate with a hypodermic needle or by popping pills. It is a certainty that you cannot smoke your way into Nirvana. The discernment between Reality and Illusion is difficult enough without giving up your faculties to a drug or a hypnotist.

The chapters on Developing Psychic Powers and Mystical Experience, then, are not road maps or instruction sheets. They are the starting points into further study.

Robert & Doris Lantz
Lafayette, New Jersey

Introduction

The Piscean age, characterized by the development of science, technology, and knowledge, has passed. A New Age has dawned. It was declared in August, 1951, that with the solar eclipse, the planet Earth had officially entered into the Aquarian Age; it was, actually, a planetary initiation as any major eclipse is. The zodiacal sign of Aquarius, ruled by the planet Uranus, dominates the next 2,000 plus year period. With the Aquarian Age, the qualities of Uranian influence and the characteristics of Aquarius will cast their force-fields over all that exists in all kingdoms on the planet Earth, symbol of the plane of dense, material matter.

The questions before mankind are: What are the influences? How will the inhabitants of Earth respond to these influences?

The Aquarian Age stresses the philosophical and humanitarian aspects of world life. Much thought and discrimination will be given to changes that are necessary in the structure and institutions of society. It should demonstrate insight into the mysteries of the Cosmos, reflected in Nature, which manifests through human, mundane affairs as well as in the lower kingdoms. Mankind will form more definite likes and dislikes concerning the world in which it lives.

Uranus, although considered cold and eccentric, in governing Aquarius, assumes humanitarian, reform movements. Change is the key-note, but, usually, rather sudden and unexpected. Investigation in the curious, inventions, etc., and interest in metaphysics, occult studies, and unusual color are ruled by Aquarius.

Now the Aquarian Age has been with us for seventeen years or more, really, and what has transpired to fulfill the promise of the New Age? We witnessed tremendous, almost earth-shattering movements by ethnic, religious, and age groups, impelled, knowingly or unknowingly, by the Uranian rays, seeking and still trying to alter the structure of society. It is as if the life-force within all manifested life, regardless of the form inhabited, were attempting to release the "ties that bind" of the past. New movements, stressing advanced thought, revolts against conservative, personal, and moral order, and interest in the mysteries of life itself predominate today.

The long-disputed science of astrology becomes enthroned after centuries of ridicule and disbelief. Gurus, meditation periods, astral investigations, developmental circles, and a plethora of seers predicting individual and world patterns are themes of today.

Metaphysics and all allied occult research attract the eagerly seeking souls throughout the world. Again, similar to the stellar science of astrology, metaphysics now enjoys an "aura of respectability." The hidden (occult) teachings of world religions are exposed to human investigation. From Tibet, India, Egypt, and other countries of the world pour the suppressed or once hidden Truths which have been maintained through countless centuries by small groups dedicated to the preservation and perpetuation of Truth.

Metaphysics is not new; it has just been "re-discovered." However, as is true in all ages, Truth has been grasped by many and abused, presenting a false, often grotesque, picture. This frightens people, interested but wary of the metaphysical approach to life. Metaphysics contains within it *all* that there is to know relating to life, its cause, its meaning, its purpose and direction. What else could mankind want but the answers to life? Metaphysics places the "philosopher's stone" into the hands of those who truly seek but stresses the fact that it is an individual matter, a personal effect and experience, for man embraces the totality of existences, of all kingdoms, of all planes. Basically, he is aware of the existence of the Truth even though his spiritual centers are unawakened.

It must be emphasized many times that each person must find his own path to the Truth. Often his way is marked in darkness and trial and error, but through effort and sacrifice, gradually, he arrives at Truth and its Light. The purpose of this writing is to present an understanding of metaphysics and metaphysical experiences. Examples of the proof of these experiences are again individual and personal. What is proof to one is not necessarily proof to another. What it does show is that it *can* and *does* happen to others. Why not to all?

Table of Contents

Man's search for Truth extends back through countless ages. The development of religions, the philosophical search for reality, the approach of science to find the answers gives testimony to the presence of inner urgings within mankind for Truth. Through all of this, a body of knowledge, metaphysics, developed to create an understanding of life and man's place in the scheme of creation. With the development has arisen many misconceptions regarding the field of metaphysics. This chapter defines, clearly, the aims and objectives of metaphysics.

The Cosmic Laws are the fabric for the manifested world, for without these Laws, there would be no existence. Cosmic Laws guide the behavior patterns of all the kingdoms from the lowest to the highest. By becoming aware and recognizing the Laws, you can better understand the externalized world around you. The cohesive forces of all manifested life is Love (harmony), the attraction between the dual principles of life, the positive and the negative. The expression of harmony in the outer self reflects inner harmony. Balance between the outer and inner selves grants you the opportunities to rise above the mundane world.

The Cosmic Influences are the powers within each of us and are available for all to contact and to use. It shows you how to gain mastery over the ever-changing situations in life. These influences are located not outside yourself, but within. They should be reflected in your qualities of character and personality; if they are not evidenced there, change your character and personality. Cosmic influences surround you, but since all of growth and learning are individual, you must learn how to locate them and how to use them. You are the "Captain of your fate, the master of your soul."

Power exists within you. Most of you realize that there is this "something other" in the created world. You tend, however, to limit it to being outside of yourselves. In reality, the power is within each of you. You must recognize the "I am" presence, use your will, and focus your attention and mind on finding Truth. Man is spiritually impoverished but wealthy, potentially. Belief and faith are necessary to the development of this power, this latent awareness within you. Once reawakened, you will never stroll through the darkness again. Self-mastery, harmony, and effort are the basic steps to attain to your Power.

You must apply the philosophy of the occult science in order to attain to Reality instead of living in the glamor of world illusion. Science has shown us the way out of many former fallacious ideas concerning physical life, and now you must find the direction in your life for real spiritual Truth, External Truth. The Truth has existed, does exist, and will always exist—with or without man's sanction—but each of you must attain to them and find balances and wholeness. The real, difficult problem is yourself. You must find yourself in the midst of today's hurry and scurry, and emplace your consciousness in the "Eternal Now" for Reality.

Each of you has, probably, sought a personal contact or union with the Ultimate and would like to know the means whereby this might be consummated. However, most of you seek it merely intellectually, for you center attentions in the realm of five senses. You must reach within to a higher consciousness. You must become "self-aware" through insight into "transcendental" knowledge. This requires detachment through self-discipline and re-direction of your thinking and behavior. Meditation periods, healthful living, proper attitudes and emotional control, and the development of patience will assist you in scaling the empyrean heights to mystical experience.

Chapter 7. MYSTICAL LIFE

Any of you can lead a mystical life. Qualifications as to age, background, education are not the criteria for your participation. It only requires your effort in studying, directing your activities, and experiencing life. By so doing, you achieve a stage of enlightenment, and your life becomes an active one. Read; be skeptical; have an open mind; seek proof as individual proof to you only. This can be done if you but cease being your own worst enemy. Help is all around you if you so decide to pursue this Mystical Life.

Chapter 8. The Way To Truth

Many of you are seeking Truth but are not aware or know the path to attain it. The Way to Truth lies within each of you, but you must find this way yourself. It cannot be located unless you are willing to apply the Cosmic Laws, to sacrifice, and to be of service to the members of all the kingdoms. It is not an easy road that promises escape from the realities of the physical world, but rather the hard road, that, in the long run, is the easy way.

Chapter 9. THE DEVELOPMENT OF PSYCHIC POWERS

Many methods exist and many groups which aim at developing your psychic powers. You must decide which method suits you, the one in which you feel the most comfortable and able to obtain the greatest results. Of all the methods, the one most endorsed by metaphysical groups is known as the Cooperative Method. This provides the logical steps by which you can open your psychic centers and tap in on the resources of powers within you. Not only is this method explained, but also directions are given for preparations of yourself and the physical area in which you will work.

MAN

&

METAPHYSICS

The seven rays are life;
all forms, the highest and the lowest, are blended together as One Body:

Joel R. Walder

BASIC METAPHYSICS

Since the beginning of time, man has sought to pierce the veil concerning the mysteries of creation in an effort to find the essence of reality. His basic questions have been: From where have I come and to where am I going? He needs an answer to arrive at a state of fulfillment within himself and to be able to intelligently work out his destiny.

In his initial stage of probing for his knowledge, he determined reality through the phenomenal (material) expression in the physical world, little realizing, then, that he saw only the Effect and not the Cause. It is through the study of practical metaphysics that man arrives at a causative stage which identifies itself with the Absolute. This must be the beginning, the Alpha of creation, and the perspective man develops here determines his spiritual progress and evolvement.

As civilization developed and man continued with his search, he soon realized that the observations of the physical, material manifestations did not contain the answers to his problem. He tried, through establishing organized religions, to finalize his quest. By image making, he postulated an idea of a god or gods which, of course, differed according to geographical location and cultural and ethnic influences.

This is why concepts of a god or gods ranged from a god of pure spirit to a god symbolized by nature and nature's forces, to a god who was as material and physical as all of life was (Greeks). Graven images were intended mainly as expressions upon which to focus thought while contemplating the formless and the invisible.

All this, then, accounts for the variances in religious establishments, all of which, regardless of place, time or culture, stemmed from an evolving awareness within man of an unknown factor in life. It is this unknown factor that has stirred man to keep inquiring about life and its reality. It all resolves itself to the fact that despite all the seeking and all the names ascribed to God, man has ever sought the reality behind all life and being. This search for Truth has been the prime factor in the evolution of mankind.

The diverse ways of searching, the varied labels given to the Absolute have caused confusion and dissidence among men, and this has been a needless expenditure of energy — spiritual, mental, and physical. In the earlier stages, had man been wiser, he would have arrived at the common denominator of Truth to delineate the Creative Force of God — regardless of the divers forms of culture, race, or historical periods.

At first, the initial religious orthodoxy seemed adequate for many people for the time and the place. However, man has grown in knowledge, perspective, and values, but few organized religions have kept pace with the advance of mankind. Man now finds he has matured and some no longer obtain satisfaction from old religions and so seek Truth in other facets or areas. He has discarded the religions which were his spiritual heritage from the past.

It is unfortunate in that by so doing, there is the danger that man might also discard the "God" contained within the old forms of religion, for in his eagerness to discover Truth, he might lose the perspective of God, which, in reality, is the Truth that is in everything. Man must see that the Universe and all therein is Truth revealed.

There seems to be a common characteristic in humanity that when man changes the structure of his society and its institutions and replaces them with new forms, he often tosses aside some of the valuable and good features of the old. It is as if any remnant of the old might contaminate the new. Often, some of the old, mingled with the new, can present a richer, a more beautiful framework in which to function. In the fervor of change, man feels offended by using some old ideas, some old terms, and determines to substitute new ideas and new names for the old.

Charles Lindberg, in the July 4, 1969, edition of LIFE magazine said it rather clearly, ". . .Through his (man's) evolving awareness, and his awareness of that awareness man can merge with the miraculous — to which we can attach what better name than 'God'?"

The present so-called gap between the ones who strive to over-throw the established systems and those who wish to retain what has always been rests on the fallacy of trying to cling to the "heritage" of form, especially in the religious areas. Man's awareness today stretches out into the infinite horizons of the universes, no longer confining itself to just the here and now. This conflict between the new school of thinking and the old can reach cataclysmic proportions and instead of solving the situation could create a society of irreconcilable opposites.

To prevent any such catastrophe, humanity must begin to revise religious concepts, yet maintaining the basic Truth that permeates them all. External features, namely, rituals, hierarchy, and physical forms, will alter to accommodate the universality of religious truth. Often it has been these externals which prevent oneness in religious belief and common understanding among the many faiths.

Of course, what is obviously faulty here in the perspective of the old and the new is the fact that their attentions *are* on externals. Few have bothered to probe deeply enough to locate the uniform Truth in all; most see only the outer manifestations which distract them. So in their thinking, *all* must go. This is wrong, for in so doing, they would destroy what man has gained (regardless of surface appearances) in spiritual evolvement.

Truth is ever Truth and no formal dress of orthodox buildings or ritualistic ceremonies can alter Truth. Spirit is the Universal Life and the substance out of which the real Universe was created. The physical, tangible world about us is but a reflection of this.

The troubled segments of man's society desire a fresher, newer presentation of the Truth of Life. Again, it must be stressed that what they are seeking already *is* and is constantly around them. If they would but wrench aside the language terminology that disturbs many, if they would but provide new channels or forms through which Truth can be expressed and explored, they, upon sincere examination, would discover wherein the Truth lies.

In the late 1950's, metaphysical leaders were given, by Higher Forces on Higher Planes, the word to initiate group movements throughout the world. Concerted efforts on the part of all these groups now in existence will, eventually, result in a general and clear understanding of what has been the "mysterious unknown" factor that man has sought. Much of the occult metaphysical teachings, maintained by small groups and dispersed sparingly to individuals, has been opened to all who earnestly seek the Truth of Life. *Now* is the New Age for Truth to be made known to mankind.

So, let us return once more to man's probing and his evolvement in this area.

The question has often been raised concerning man and his relation to the Universe and all that resides within that Universe. He ponders over the thought that if man did *not* exist, would all else in the manifested Universe still be? This reminds one of the story of a forest of trees, one of which crashed, in a storm, to the earth, but there was no one in the forest at that time. Since no one was there to hear it, was there a sound from the crash? Of course there was! Man, again, must realize that there is a reality and there is illusion. Too often, he concentrates on illusion and is caught in a web of delusion.

It is certainly true that the reality of the here and now is more with us than that of the past.

"What is" is a result of the evolved awareness in the human consciousness and this awareness is possible for all the created beings throughout all of the universes.

Reality can never be more than a fragmentary revelation of the Mind of God, for the world exhibits itself merely as the immediate presence of the Absolute, but not of its nature. The nature of the Cosmic, the ultimate source of everything, is the most difficult, the most complex problem we could face. We observe just the outer, the active aspect of God in the manifested world, but the inner, passive qualities elude us and our observations. Reality must rest upon the idea of the Universe being an outcome of Divine Ideation (thought). In other words, all that was, is, and ever shall be is but a thought contained in the Mind of the Great Oversoul (God). So, what man really sees as Reality is but a projection of the Mind of God.

However, all of the approaches to an understanding of Reality are involved and, often, confusing to the average man's mind. It is not important, actually, what approach we use to establish Reality. Man seeks it in order to comprehend it, not just intellectually, but as a way to improve life in all of its daily aspects.

How can man find or approach Reality? As stated previously, his religions have failed to provide him with the answer. Notice that "the means" was not stated, for all of the religions contain within themselves the "means" to find the answer.

Men of science have attempted an approach. But the realm of science can be equally confusing, for can the average person grasp the immensity of the 100,000,000 galaxies so far discovered and observed through the telescopes? Does man realize the structure of the atom? Is the DNA Factor comprehensible by each man? Every day new things are being discovered in all fields of endeavor, but does man understand fully? Religions use symbols; the sciences employ terminology, but neither seems to suffice for man to find Reality.

Still, man continues his search for the answers from where he originated, what his purpose is here, and where he is going. The search leads him to investigate varied realms of thought, all approaches possible, all schools of belief. Remember that the origin of religions is based upon man's attempt to comprehend the forces behind natural phenomena. In so doing, he ascribed Divine Powers to these forces. This was his primitive stage in investigation, and as he evolved in his knowledge, so did his concepts and his search through the religions. At first, religious law or tenets served man, but as he developed and observed life, he replaced these ancient taboos with the knowledge and with scientific laws of that time.

Ages passed and man's knowledge increased; science provided more principles as well. Religions seemed to be in danger of being overshadowed by science, for men relied less and less upon religion to find the answer to his questions. Civil law dominated religious law and the authorities within the churches relinquished certain controls to civil authority or were, at least, forced to recognize civil law. Science seemed to become the dominant force in life.

Yet, man soon found out that science could not supply the answers either, for what man seeks and still seeks falls not only in the realm of science. The classification of spiritual things resides in an area apart, in which the spiritual forces move and have their being.

It seems rather strange that man has accomplished so much, scientifically and materially, and yet has not reached the basic answers to the questions which disturbed him from primitive times to the present.

Could it be that man has concentrated all his efforts in seeking the reasons behind Reality in the external or material features of life and has neglected to recognize that the Reality he seeks is in the invisible world? Also, if man would but look to nature and to himself, he might locate the solution so long eluded. The final contest of mankind is man!

By turning within, man soon discovered that all the knowledge he had acquired through the eons of living still did not offer him the means of really understanding himself or life. Man cannot take scientific systems to explain himself, but there are other sources that could assist him. The truth, actually, lies within all the old laws and teachings. These can be found if one searches back to the pure origin of religions — not in the concepts as handed down from the pulpits today. The purity and essence of Truth in all religions became corrupted through ritual, hierarchial authority with its ego-centered interpretation of Law and Truth.

The old, original, and pure Truths are still there but carefully concealed. Perhaps 95% of humanity are unaware of the existence of these Truths because of the fact that they still look to the externals of religion — not to the causative elements behind each religion.

Much of this concealment was purposeful, for there is Truth of Great Power contained in the ancient teachings. In the hands of the wrong people (church officials as well) much harm could result. The White Magic (good forces) and the Black Magic (negative forces) both have their basis in the same laws. One represents the correct use of Truth; the other, its abuse.

Also, it is only common sense to conceal basic Truth until man proves his ability to understand and to use it properly. One does not start a five year old child in the ninth grade. Knowledge comes in a series of progressive experiences, with each successive experience based on the preceeding one.

It is the study of metaphysics (occult) which opens the door to the recognition, the awareness, and the acceptance of true Reality. However, few have been exposed to this study in the past—again, carefully guarded and sparingly granted to tested individuals through the centuries. It is the New Age which has rendered the veil of secrecy in this work and has offered it to the multitudes. By its very nature, metaphysical knowledge contains sufficient safeguards to prevent mass abuse, but there is some misuse nevertheless.

Unfortunately, as is true in all group movements in all ages of man's history, there have been some who assume the interest and sincerity of desire to *know*. They have, through misuse of ego, utilized metaphysical knowledge to promote themselves rather than the Truth. In this New Age, there has developed an overabundance of self-styled gurus, seers, predictors (psychic) of world events, etc. Crowds rely upon their words, change their lives according to the dictates of these misguiding leaders. The teachings extended by these "teachers", in essence, disprove them, but their followers see only the external personality of the "guru" and have not their attention on the essentials of Truth.

However, all of this is good for now. At least, the masses of mankind are closer to and have been exposed to the Reality of Truth. They, actually, are on the right path to finding the answers. As each person becomes more aware and develops this awareness, he will awaken to the realization that these are the "false prophets", and he will discover that Reality exists within the teachings and, above all, within himself. Man will, eventually, depersonalize leadership and attend only to the Laws and Truths given to him.

The history of metaphysics is as ancient as creation, for metaphysics stresses the Causative Principle and has been the body of knowledge maintained by the Higher Forces. It has been the school of learning kept by certain assigned groups throughout the ages in each civilization. Egypt had a group of priests known as inner priests, who guarded the ancient teachings. Aknaton was the pharaoh who successfully passed the occult initiations given by the inner priests, and it was he who, realizing the one great unity underlying the universe, tried to convert Egypt to a monotheistic religion. He failed not only because the outer priests feared that their secure positions and the hold they had over the people were in jeopardy, but also because the time was not ripe. There were not enough advanced people yet ready for this.

The Greeks had the Eleusian mystery schools. Remember it was Alcibiades who had to flee to Syracuse because he had revealed some of these mysteries to others not yet ready for them. The Zorastrians, the Hebrews (Kabala), and the early Christians had the hidden mystery schools. Buddhism as is taught and practiced today is quite different from the mystical Buddhism which is the basis of the Buddhist faith. Throughout the ages the mystery schools have persisted, and it is through the metaphysical knowledge, maintained by those groups through the centuries, that the Cosmic Truth is being dispensed to earth's inhabitants at this time.

Now, what is occult metaphysics? We are concerned here with the metaphysics which is related to the study of that which is beyond the physical, external manifestations of all that is. It goes to the heart, the core of everything—not only on the physical plane, but also on all the Higher planes. It explains Truth and Reality on all the planes of life.

This sounds very complicated and complex—perhaps too deep for the average person. How long a time would be needed and how much educational background would be necessary to learn it all? Time is unimportant, for the Cosmic is spaceless and timeless, and man has an eternity in which to accomplish this and has his successive incarnations to learn each Law and Truth. This he does through his experiences. Educational background does not enter the picture, for understanding and perspective are based on awareness, which will develop out of man's experiences in life. Knowledge gained by experience brings greater knowledge more often than just the mere accumulation of facts.

True, many metaphysical concepts are not easy to grasp nor easy to accept. It is advisable for anyone who studies metaphysics (occult) to observe these rules: Be skeptical—accept nothing as Reality or Truth until it is proved; Keep an open mind to the possibility that it could be so; Be sincere in seeking Truth, and it will be proved. Effort in the application of metaphysical Laws and Truths is necessary for the proof to evidence itself to the person. Reject nothing; accept nothing, but in the sincerity of the person's effort to find Truth, pieces of the puzzle soon begin to fall into place.

The first step in metaphysical knowledge is to become aware of oneself and one's soul qualities. This requires that man must alter his life, must develop greater understanding, will accept the individual responsibility of himself and his daily living experiences. In order to accomplish this, he has to apply his efforts in learning and control his emotions and thought patterns. His development in all this must be a steady but slow one; it should not be rapid. Soul awareness or consciousness is not a result of quick developmental methods, but rather a slow process involving much hard work and consistent application of Cosmic Laws to everyday life.

Many misconceptions prevail concerning the nature of occultism, and these act as deterrents to many who might benefit from the knowledge. Occult metaphysics does not fall into the category of magic, although both magic and occultism begin at the same point of origin, employ the identical terminology, methods, and laws. However, all of life is a matter of duality and polarity. Occult metaphysics and magic are the opposing forces of this polarity, but still represent a common factor—man's transcendental consciousness. By transcendental consciousness is meant that which goes beyond everyday physical and material conscious experiences.

The goal of occult metaphysics is to grant to all created things the opportunity to grow mentally and spiritually by transcending the world of the physical senses. In so doing, the identity or self of each unit of creation unites with the One, the Eternal, the Absolute. In the human kingdom this is the common goal in man's development; in the lower kingdoms it is similar but an inherent, instinctive drive.

Magic is self-centered in that it seeks to draw all things to itself in a possessive manner. The *will*, in magic, attempts only to attain to what is termed "super-sensible" knowledge, but the real intellect is not involved.

In the final analysis, occult metaphysics strives to eliminate individuality, for it rests on a premise of non-individuality, attempting to transcend the limitations which accompany individuality. The ultimate goal of occult metaphysics is the surrender of the individual to Ultimate Reality, which is accomplished through the element of perfectly balanced Harmony (Love). Harmony stems from the heart, the real source of life's energy. When the heart is mentioned, most people think of it from the viewpoint of emotional love, but in occult metaphysics, reference to the heart means the center of pure Harmony and the seat of the "seed atom", which is the central or core atom of the individual, which each lifetime incarnates, carrying with it the sum total of all the person's individual evolvements or regressions from all his incarnations.

It is not meant to imply here that occult metaphysics denies the passions or the emotions, for man must feel deeply when performing in life. Thought, for example, is a powerful force, but it requires the feeling behind it to give it the energy or momentum needed to be effective.

Metaphysics serves as a guide for man to explore his worlds, the visible and the invisible, and himself. Although the guidelines (Laws and Truths) are established for man to pursue, they are not the be-all or the end-all in metaphysics, for it remains that the personal experiences finalize man's evolvement and development spiritually. It is the intent of occult metaphysics not only to know about, but also "to be."

Ultimately, occult metaphysics hopes to lead man to that conscious union with the ever-present, ever-living Absolute. It is the Divine Spark within man that seeks this reunion, for the Divine Spark descended into matter from pure Spirit, was individualized in man as Soul, and yearns for this conscious union, which is personal and complete.

The Absolute is "Now" and it is "Now" that is so important in man's progress to perceive transcendental Reality. The Reality resides within all and has been experienced by all in many ways in daily living—when man loves, when he feels compassion for someone in difficulty, when he becomes immersed in beautiful music to the exclusion of all else around him. When man projects himself into a beautiful painting of a landscape or a seascape, he touches Divine Reality. All these examples show something of the unknown factor that humanity leans toward.

Cosmic importance has always been given to the great classical music, for it assists man to transcend the earthly conditions, temporarily, and stimulates responses in him to the pulsation of universal movement. Beethoven has been considered the greatest of all the musicians in bringing the "music of the spheres" down to the ears of humanity. This "music of the spheres" is the Voice of Reality, and anyone who has encountered this music in meditation periods knows what is implied here.

Symbols find an important role in occult metaphysics, for symbols stimulate imagery and communicate Truth, not literal Truth, but suggestive Truth. There are volumes that have been written on the symbology in occult metaphysics, but unless one has a proper background in the knowledge of the subject, many fallacious interpretations arise. For, again, symbols are meaningful to the individual depending upon what he is and where he is on the ladder of evolution. Proof and meaning of symbols remain an individual experience.

Common concepts of occult metaphysics often relegated it to a realm of peculiarities, oddities in thought and to those who delved into its study. The consensus resolved occult metaphysicians as little old, white-haired ladies, dressed in flowing robes, who

simpered platitudinous phrases. They were the busy-bodies who in-
serted their beliefs into everyone else's life.

This is a far cry from the real metaphysician. He is from all
walks of life, from every economic, social, and educational level,
from all races and both sexes. A true metaphysician is "active calmly, and calmly active" and practical in all he does, for metaphysics
is not something only to ponder over or to observe. True, its goal is
transcendental and the spiritualization of all of life in its totality.
The core of attention is upon the Ultimate Reality and attempts active union as a state of being through an expanded awareness or
consciousness.

Metaphysics does not teach that this state of being is arrived at
merely by contemplation or by emotional involvements with the
ideals of the Truth or Laws. The spiritual progress in occult
metaphysics is difficult, for man has to change his habitual, old
modes of thinking and doing, has to remold his character and personality, has to awaken his consciousness and develop his
awareness through this. Man then has to try to identify with the Absolute, demonstrating the Law of Identification as the Reality.

Those who follow occult metaphysical teachings know that
their attainment will be a personal and individual one based upon
the experiences in daily life. The Rosicrucian Order (A.M.O.R.C.)
teaches that all knowledge is based upon experience, and man cannot attain unless he knows. As man acts in life, responding to conditions according to the knowledge he has gleaned, he sees results.

For what does occult metaphysics feel man should be acting?
Man's actions, physical and mental, should be a conscious effort to
surmount the plane of physical desires and achieve a spiritual life
while dwelling on the physical plane. This requires effort. Some
hope to achieve this through study only, but nothing is gained completely by this. Developing a certain skill in metaphysical work does
not bring spiritual fulfillment either. Also, there exist many who
possess great knowledge in metaphysics, but that is all that they
possess.

The study of occult metaphysics is important, for a person
must have a foundation upon which to act. However, too many confine their metaphysical study only to its perusal. Man cannot really
know metaphysics unless the Law of Application is followed, for
one does not really know until he has experienced.

The New Age, again, brought forth those who developed skills
in mediumship, psychism, E.S.P., etc. but as one observes many of
these people, one can detect that all they know is that particular
skill and nothing more. Mediums are too plentiful today, but few

are knowledgeable in occult metaphysics and tend to mislead and dispense false information. Less than 1% of the mediums and psychics today are reliable sources for those who seek the way to Reality.

Knowledge alone serves only to expose a person to the occult metaphysical world. There are many here, too, who have studied much, but understand little, mouthing the usual cliches in the field and, thus, appearing to be quite advanced. These people are easy to discern, for as each individual develops and learns on his own, he can detect the superficiality of those who possess knowledge but not the understanding.

A few years ago, a gentleman joined a metaphysical group in New Jersey. He was quite brilliant (two college degrees), had a fine vocabulary, and seemed very well-read in the metaphysical areas. At first, the group felt that he would contribute much, but as time passed, it became very evident that what he knew was but a surface knowledge. His actions became rather obnoxious as he attempted to force his opinions upon others; he also would not listen to the ideas or thoughts that others had. In conversations, he was able to latch on to another's thought as it was being expressed, and he would then insert phrases that prompted others to feel he knew all about the subject. Time adjusts and balances all things. Within a year, he found he could no longer dominate others in their thoughts. In a short time, he "weeded" himself out of the group; no one had to say or to do anything, but the Law worked.

Knowledge is fine and excellent to possess, and study should help in the metaphysical endeavor. However, it is understanding that is more important, but that, too, can be augmented by study and the application of the knowledge gained. Knowledge just for the sake of knowledge is not sufficient.

Why do people study metaphysics? Some do it for selfish reasons or because it is different and open for argument or is an intellectual challenge or thought provoking. True metaphysicians do not look for personal reward from the standpoint of attention from others. It is a paradox in metaphysics that one finds satisfaction because he does not seek it and fulfills his personality by the very nature of renouncing it.

Metaphysicians are realists and do not dwell in illusions; the glamor of the world and its material objects are placed in their proper values. Temporal events, places, things are illusory facets of physical life and not of Reality in the sense of permanence. Metaphysics teaches that there is but one Reality — Spirit — and that is eternal. It demonstrates, too, that that something implicit within the self and in the Universe is the Eternal Spirit—all that was, is, and ever will be.

Plotinus declared that the Absolute is present in all things even though man might be unaware that It is so.

Man should contemplate upon the inner faculties of his soul, for it is that part of the Divine Spark which he has individualized through the learning experiences of all his incarnations. Man is a universe within himself and should develop his Self to reveal the In-dwelling Presence of the Deity. Perhaps man should cease to consider himself and all the physical world as a though projected out of the Over-Soul, but should see himself as part of the Cosmic Substance immersed in the world of matter to learn and experience on that plane of existence.

It is man's purpose in life to develop the God qualities which are latent within him. By surmounting the physical desires, by losing his individuality, by developing his soul-consciousness and living from the heart center, man can transcend the world of the physical senses and become One with the All. To accomplish this, man must experience *all* of life, being excused from not one example of living, and by this experiencing, he *knows*. "And the Truth shall make you free."

Metaphysics emphasizes that all of creation has its origin from the Universal Mind—World Mind—The Absolute—God. Man must become aware of his Divine heritage, the Reality of his existence. In so doing, he then can visualize the world in its proper perspective; the glamor and illusions disappear. Then, man sees that all that "is" has purpose and all is "becoming". Nothing exists by chance or for-tune, nor does anything remain inactive. All is vibrating, expanding, ever-growing. Matter is always "becoming"; so is Truth.

Metaphysics is not just a body of knowledge exclusively set aside for a few who are educated. It is for any person who sincerely desires to improve himself, to change his way of life for the better, fo find a way to believe in something that is true and real. People who so desire indicate, also, that they are willing to alter their lives, for involvement in metaphysics *will* change a person's life and, usually, for the better depending on how the person uses metaphysical knowledge. Their thoughts, their emotions will undergo alterations as well. Most of these people have floundered in life, following whatever way has been presented to them—almost as if they were tumble weeds being blown in all directions by the variable winds.

The study of metaphysics shows to man that there is a way of life which can bring him satisfaction in developing the spiritual side of life and bring him closer to Reality. It promises a glimpse of that unknown factor and an assurance that can be a permanent fixture in man's life. Also, there are those who can attest to the validity of all this, for they have had the experience of it. These people can be detected and tested easily, for their lives are an example and a reflection of the Truths and the Laws.

Those who engage in the study of metaphysics will soon notice how their lives have changed, and often this will be a drastic change. This should not deter anyone, for the results are most rewarding in that the daily life experiences become amazingly easy, for man then knows *the why* of his existence and for all manifested creation. Life becomes more orderly, more meaningful, fuller and richer in experiences and in satisfactions. The problems of living no longer disturb him, for he learns the Law of Acceptance and realizes that he is where he is meant to be, for he put himself there in the first place by virtue of his past incarnations. He now knows that the "job at hand" is the important one, and he knows just what that is also. By so knowing, he can complete the job, learn the lessons contained therein and the disciplines involved. Through all trials and tribulations, he can carry on because he knows that in the end, all will be right.

Involvement in metaphysical study gives direction in life, for, at least, man then knows where he is going. He realizes that he has his own individual life and challenges to meet, and through them he learns the lessons he needs to develop spiritually. The temporary, illusory material world no longer is the Reality for him. He finds his true identity by becoming aware of his Higher Self which dwells within—often referred to as the "Indwelling Presence". This is his real inheritance in life, but it remains for man to stimulate his faculties to become more aware of it. In becoming aware of it and realigning his thoughts, feelings, and actions to a harmonious balance within this Higher Self, he can live in the Eternal "Now".

How can man arrive at this awareness, this state of being in which he can live from the center of the Higher Self? First, metaphysical instructions state that man must be evolved to the point where he is ready and willing to learn, to accept something new and seemingly different. Since man has from the beginning of time sought this apparently elusive "unknown beyond", he should be more than willing to work for it. Doubts and fears will exist, but knowing that *it is there* should dispel them. It should always be remembered that this is a personal experience for each individual. So, each upon the discovery of a new way of life and light should be courageous enough and believe strongly enough to move toward it.

In so doing, it will invoke the Law of Attraction and bring more and more of it to him.

Just what is it that occult metaphysics grants to those who embark on this path? There are many things that result from contact with and application of metaphysical Truths. First, man will obtain an inner enlightenment, the goal of so many in today's world. Secondly, it brings Reality in its essence to man's consciousness. Thirdly, man learns how to live differently with new ideals, new values, new perspectives which give him a constructive, purposeful life. Fourthly, there is a personal reaction or satisfaction gained through all of the experiences of a metaphysical life with the knowledge of attainment and development.

The results of metaphysical living will bring calmness out of chaos. It gives direction, a practical philosophy of living that really works. Life assumes a more pleasant hue and is no longer subject to periods of depression, moodiness, or being in the doldrums of despair. Since all things now are seen in their proper perspective, there no longer exists any excuse for melancholy or negativism in any way.

Living metaphysically needs no definition. Terminology or description of any kind is not necessary. All it takes is living it and being the example to others. Metaphysicians do not attempt to force their opinions or beliefs upon others, but feel rather that by example, others will see and might then be interested enough to try it also. Then, others will know that the metaphysical life is really very simple, very practical.

People wonder if occult metaphysics causes conflicts with their religious beliefs. There is no need for concern here, for occult metaphysics recognizes that all religions have their basis in mystical experiences. It recognizes the validity of Truth underlying and behind all the constructive religions of the world. These Truths are the common denominator pervading all religions. It is taught that he who pursues the metaphysical path becomes a better Christian, a better Jew, a better Buddhist, for this study emphasizes belonging to a religious group, but with a difference. By virtue of the metaphysical teachings, man reverses his attitudes towards his religion in that now he will want to give instead of always receiving. He brings understanding and more of himself to his religion and *asks little* in return. Before participating in metaphysics, man was prone to ask for something from his religion, from his God, always seeking their solution for *his problems. As a metaphysician, man learns to stand on his own two*feet, find his own solutions to the problems which he created in the first place. Since he set the situation into motion, he was the creator and now has the responsibility to mitigate the circumstances. There is always help from the Higher Forces, but the initial effort must first be made by man, the originator of the problems in life.

Through metaphysical study, life becomes easier, and each person finds himself more at ease, more contented, for all problems are placed in their proper categories. It is not intended here to promote the idea of "ease" in metaphysical living, for, in actuality, it becomes a more active life. Once exposed to the Laws and Truths, man has the responsibility of applying them to his life. Life is not viewed as easy so much as calmness in the midst of turmoil and confusion. Instead of exciting activity, it is an interesting activity, for man is thrown into the throes of the mundane world, but the approach is different, the rewards very satisfying and permanent. Now, instead of being a so-called victim of the physical world of the senses, man becomes its master. Mastership of self brings mastership over the exigencies of life.

Next, what is the group stressing in its search? Do they seek and investigate all avenues of Truth, or do they seem to concentrate or specialize on one aspect? Do they take the Laws and Truths from all schools of thought or simply follow what one school advocates?

To become a true metaphysician, man must see that his life, to that point, has been an illusory one, with his attentions solely upon the externals, upon the sense-perceptive world. Most of his activity has been geared from the Lower Self, the physical or animal man. Humanity must first learn to live from the center of the Higher Self and to transmute the energies of the Lower Self into higher qualities.

How can this be achieved? The desire to develop spiritually must be present and the willingness to change his ways of thinking, believing, and acting. Naturally, help or guidelines are needed, for one does not cast off the old modes of living without having a substitute available. Study is necessary. But what does one study and to what degree can he be certain that he is studying the right thing?

There are many reputable, established metaphysical orders that teach the Cosmic Laws and Truths. Membership in these groups assists in the initial stages, for their work is organized and progressive. Caution is stressed in that it must be remembered that no one group has a monopoly on Truth. Any organization that declares it has the only way should be approached with hesitation.

Compare life to a wheel, the hub of which is the center of strength and the goal. The mass of humanity is the rim of the wheel, and the paths to the hub (Truth) are the spokes. Does it matter what spoke a person travels along so long as it is constructive and leads to the ultimate good?

Group membership is another way to the study of occult metaphysics, but this can be the most dangerous, and the most frustrating of all. These groups exist everywhere today, and when each person is ready, the Law of Attraction functions. Before long, a newspaper article on a metaphysical group will come to his attention or a passing statement by someone will alert him to the presence of a group within his vicinity.

But, the question remains concerning the validity of the group's teachings, their aims and objectives. Here it becomes a matter of personal discrimination. A person should meet with the group and observe the following:

Does the leader seem to occupy a central position of personal adulation on the part of his audience? Does he exude a know-it-all attitude? Does he call upon members of the group for information? Is he in front of what he teaches or simply behind it, acting only as a channel for what Truth he has learned and is *sharing* his experiences with others?

Over the past twenty years, there have been so many groups organized, but they have been short-lived. The Egos of those in charge prevented continuation of the group work. Flying Saucer groups in New York City, metaphysical study groups, self-development groups have flourished and expired because of this factor-ego domination.

Now, how does the group operate? Is there a flavoring of organized organization? Too often goals become bogged down by the wheels of organizational methods. The best working groups contain a minimal amount of organization—only what is necessary to arrange the meetings and to have the facilities. All else will fall into an orderly fashion without dictatorial methods. It seems almost too casual sometimes, but it more often than not functions more smoothly and has greater and longer lasting continuity.

Is there a great deal of ritual? Do the ceremonial aspects, the wearing of apparel, the stress of incantations seem to be too prevalent? The best conducted sessions and study groups ignore the ritualistic ceremonies and are simple and plain in operation. Truth is ever Truth and needs no dressing or preparation for acceptance.

Next, what is the group stressing in its search? Do they seek and investigate all avenues of Truth, or do they seem to concentrate or specialize on one aspect? Do they take the Laws and Truths from all schools of thought or simply follow what *one* school advocates?

About fifteen years ago, a metaphysical group met and enjoyed a fine rapport among all of its members and was searching through all literature and all schools. A segment within the group felt it had to break off and to investigate on its own. They did so, but confined their search to the phenomenal aspect. Table knocking was very prominent in their meetings, and from all information known to-date, they are still knocking tables, but have gone no further.

Another phase to look for is the attitude each participating member has for every other member. Is there a feeling or atmosphere of ease? Do they accept others who are new and not so knowledgeable? Do they respect each other's opinions—even those who disagree with some of the teachings? Do they *share* their personal experiences with one another? Also, is there a good sense of humor present? It does not have to be an air of complete solemnity and seriousness, for life and the Laws and Truth are meant to be enjoyed in a wholsome manner.

What is the reading material present or suggested by the group? Is it varied to accommodate varied tenets? Does it encompass as many aspects of occult metaphysics as possible? Do they inform the readers to be selective and discriminative in the readings, or does any one author, any one book contain *all* the way?

Is money a dominant feature? Is there an amount charged to meet expenses or is there an element of profit? It is a truism in life that man is suspicious of and values little what comes to him for nothing. Nominal fees should exist, but should not go beyond this. A short time ago, a group invited an outside speaker who came from a distance. The fee was $1.00 per person which took care of expenses and gave a little profit. It is unfortunate that the speaker was overheard, after the lecture, saying, "We've got our money; let's go!" Many might have been interested in a group which he lead in another area, but that statement destoryed all interest. Of itself, money is not an evil. It is the things which might be done with money that cause evil.

With all these questions before him, one can, sooner or later, find the group which will be best for *him*. Perhaps he will continue with it for a long period or stay just long enough to prepare himself for another group. Perhaps the person will find that he gains more through just study, but this is the weakest approach, for group membership and group discussion can be instrumental in clarification of ideas. Man needs an outside influence to see Truth from another approach.

Above all, man must seek Truth where he *feels*, within himself, comfortable and that the truth sounds reasonable and just— to him. What is necessarily Truth to one does not have to be Truth to another. This is conditioned by each one's personal experiences in life and where each one is on the levels of evolvement. Remember that Truth, as matter, is always "becoming."

Today, the presses pour out metaphysical books, astrology books, for man has become acutely conscious that occult metaphysics contains the answers to the long sought question of his origin, his purpose, his direction. However, do all of these books serve to instruct man properly?

As in an age in any cycle of events, there are those who leap on the bandwagon of the current interest— not so much to enhance man's knowledge but to benefit monetarily. There is a wide selection of literature on the market for man to choose from. Caution again is advised, for many of the do-it-yourself books in this field can be dangerous. Books advocating self-development of psychic powers, astral projections, six easy lesson astrological guides are all pathetically mediocre, but more than that, are dangerous and harmful.

None of this type should be read until a person has read, sufficiently and wisely, the literature that is qualified to prepare for him a solid foundation in metaphysical Truth. Most of the authors of the do-it-yourself form of writing are unschooled in the metaphysical teachings and have no idea as to what they are stating. They have no business advising others on how to do what they themselves have never done.

Anyone interested in engaging in occult metaphysics should carefully observe the foregoing guide when it involves joining a group for study purposes. The person should remember, however, that regardless of existing conditions, it all depends upon himself, the sincerity of his purpose, the motives behind his desires to evolve spiritually. All of life is individual; growth is individual; learning is individual. Out of any group participation can come much according to what the person puts into it and on what his attention is.

Metaphysical life is for anyone who so desires it and makes the proper effort. It is not limited nor belongs exclusively to any group—economic, social, religious or ethnic. Taking part in meatphysical living depends only upon the strength of the desires within each person. Continued involvement would be determined by the degree of application of metaphysical Laws and Truths that the person attempts. He must develop a good insight along with the knowledge he acquires and realize that all which comes his way is beneficial—if not now, then later.

The word "detachment" frequently appears in metaphysical works. This can cause confusion for many could take it literally and completely, and this is now what is meant by the use of the word. It is true that metaphysics aims at detaching ourselves from the dominion of the physical senses, but metaphysics does *not* and *never* has denied the purposeful place of the senses in the material world. It acknowledges that through the sense perceptive faculties and the experiences gained therefrom, man grows through the learning experiences and continues until he is no longer dominated by but rather controls his sense desires.

There are those who attach themselves to this word and fail to recognize its true meaning. By detachment, to them, they feel that the way is to deny the senses, to deny the world, to deny themselves participation in worldly life. This is not correct from a true metaphysical sense.

Man must be involved in the physical world with all the appurtenances of physical living. That is why he is here. Spirit must experience all of the gross matter events in order to subject or transmute the forces of matter to the Higher Self. Eventually, the state of "desireless desire" is reached by every advanced spiritualized being, but to reach this state, each must have tasted the wines of desire.

Detachment implies that man no longer is ruled by the physical senses, no longer places his attention and values on *just* material things (homes, money, position, cars, etc). He knows the importance of everything and realizes that he must propel himself into the mundane world to experience and to know and to share this with others. Detachment does *not* mean to give up all material things completely but to use them properly and to put them in a proper perspective.

Man forgets that homes can be replaced if destroyed; money can be gained again by effort; life is continuous and does not end at death. So why hold such a firm grip on these "things"? This is where detachment comes in, for if a person loses all, he knows he can regain it if necessary, but life does not cease from loss of material things or those close to him. A true mystic does not sink into the depths of despair when all is lost around him, but aloofly surveys the wreckage, knowing why it happened, accepting it, and proceeding along in life.

In metaphysics man is told that he cannot alter the past, for what is done is done. The present is the "now" in which he moves and has his being and is a product of the past and is that which conditions his future.

Man must fix attention on living calmly, and thus he will attain the goals which will grant him great rewards. He must become aware of the Higher Force within him, ally himself with sources of assistance — a book, a teacher, a group.

The mysteries of life are solved when man perceives all planes of consciousness and that all people are on different levels. Metaphysics tells man that Spirit, the Universal Life, is the substance out of which the real universe is created and that the material world is but a reflection of this Spirit. In following the metaphysical Truths, the whole of man's life improves. It is all very simple, really.

COSMIC LAWS

There are so many questions that apparently school, science, philosophy and religion have not answered.

Why does there seem to be such injustice? The people who push ahead and take and shove have what appear to be the luxuries of life. He who does not—because he believes everyone should have a chance—and holds back, seems to not get ahead, even to suffer a great deal more. "Too bad that had to happen to so-and-so, he was always such a nice person."

Can it be that there is a reason, something that we have not been told about. . . some kind of secret. . . what about thoughts. . . what is the power of positive thinking?

Cosmic law demonstrates itself in all areas of living, material as well as spiritual. All that has been, or ever will be is a manifestation of the Cosmic Law at work. Although you view certain phases or portions of life as being a section of a "great unknown" there is, actually, nothing mysterious about any segment of the two worlds. Your not knowing these Cosmic Laws makes it appear as if there is a mystery to the Universe, but the Cosmos never intended that any portion of the World Mind or Infinite Intelligence and the knowledge contained within it would be withheld from you.

One of the basic Cosmic Laws is "All is in all," and as each of you is a material member of the creation, whatever is is within you and in everything else. You have but to find the way to become aware of this oneness that pervades the Universe. All *is* One! However, the contact with this universality of the dual existences must be yours.

Perhaps it is difficult for you to grasp, for it seems so strange that whatever is within you also exists throughout all the kingdoms and all the Universes. The astronomer, Dr. Strumberg, in his book, THE SOUL OF THE UNIVERSE, stated there exists everywhere in the Universe a similarity, a unity, and he mentions that so long as this unity presents itself, you should accept the fact that there is a Unifying Agent. This Unifying Agent and the universal commonness emphasize that whatever exists in one place, exists elsewhere and in all things.

The present upheavals on the part of different ethnic groups and age levels is merely an attempt to discover and to unify all the segments of society and the planet into One—a cohesive, working, single unit—Spirit functioning through the physical world. It is unfortunate that these attempts by various groups employ methods which seem to disintegrate the structure of society rather than to unite them. These groups of the New Age Thought have responded to the vibratory rate of the Aquarian Age, but might lose what they have attained within their consciousness by wrong methods and listening to the ever-present "false prophets". The "rebels" as they are termed, really have latched on to the central theme or objective of the Aquarian Age, but they need to *know* more of what and why they are striving for.

The theme of Oneness, Love, Peace, and Unity substantiates the Law of All is in all. Arguments presented against this, center around physical form life in the human, animal, vegetable, and mineral kingdoms. What you are concerned with here is *life*, and life exists throughout the galaxies but not necessarily as you, in your limited scope of knowledge and understanding, conceive of it to be. Life is not the form but the energy or the force that activates it.

Galactic systems exist not through caprice of the Creator or by chance. Chance, in itself, would imply great divergence in behavioral patterns within the systems. Since scientists agree that everything follows a cyclic pattern in the Universe—planets remain in their orbits at a steady pace of movement and rotation, certain comets appear with regularity, etc.—then, you have to agree that there has been a causative element, an intelligence behind it all. In metaphysics it is stated that, "In the beginning, God geometrized." The consistency and regularity of planetary functioning should lead you to think deeply about that metaphysical tenet.

This regularity follows down into the life patterns here on earth—seasons come and go, night follows day, etc. Within all kingdoms, the pattern continues in cyclic fashion. Could all this be a product of a chance event, or does it imply an intelligence that has set forth the motion and gives it Laws and Truths to guide it?

Just review your own life from this thought! Looking back, hasn't there been cyclic patterns in your periods of growth, learning, and experiencing? From birth to death, the major happenings in your life will seem to carry a repetitious aspect. Of course, once you learn a lesson, that does not have to be subject to the repetition. However, how many of us really learn the lessons of living? And so, the repeating goes on and on.

It also follows that whatever exists within the Universe and within you can be contacted or become yours. Here it is implied more the spiritual, but as the Law functions, the material, as well, is based on the spiritual ("As above, so below"). The material, physical demonstration of tangible life is but a reflection of the spiritual life made manifest on this plane of existence.

So you again can postulate that anything in the created Universe can be yours. To obtain it, you must desire it, and the intensity of the desire determines when and how much you can possess. There is the Law of Responsibility, and what you desire is subject to this Law. Individual responsibility for what you are and where you are going serves as a precautionary factor in setting forth your wishes.

The responsibility necessitates that what you desire should be most constructive and positive, for the Law of Cause and Effect, once stimulated into your life according to the quality of your desires. By this action, you become the Creator of your life, for you initiate the basic forces of the events in your environment.

Negative desires reach fulfillment also, for the Law operates everywhere in the positive and negative portions of being. All of life is duality; nothing exists solely as one element. Polarity and the Law of Opposites remain the basis of all. Desiring negative things can bring you what you wish, but look for accompanying responsibility. These responsibilities will later affect you in discord, failure, illness, for the Law of Cause and Effect follows, and you have energized negative forces.

About two years ago, I was discussing the Cosmic Supply and stated that it was available to all if you have faith enough and put forth the effort in the right direction. An individual who had many children and, thus, many responsibilities remarked that it is easy for those without families to claim this. He is very religious and active as a member of his church. I said that the BIBLE declares this as well—the Lord provides—and Jesus attested to this Truth when he fed the multitudes. Faith is the key, but, of course, you must work rightly and with the proper attitudes. When you do this, the Cosmic Supply becomes available in the form of opportunities, and often as a reward for correct action and correct thinking.

Believe it is so and it will be for you. This is true on all planes of life, but you must place your attention on what you want, have faith, put forth the effort, and what you desire is yours.

The Absolute intends that there is enough of everything for all of you and, especially, of all that is of value. God's dominion over all life resides within you, for you are his creation and contain within you the same power to create. Your inability to create is only because you do not know how to use this power. Of course, you must first become aware of the authority which you have latent within you. As a part of the Creator, you are capable of a higher sphere of activity, and you embrace all things and yet are higher than all.

Recognition of the Higher Forces within you is the determining factor. You have to arrive at the state of awareness in which you Know that you possess the same creative Higher Forces. Christ said, "Go to the temple within," implying the God-force resident within you. You have your body as the externalized illustration of the Higher Forces, and you should always remind yourself that the body is not you, but yours. The body is just the channel through which you function.

The body and the externalized personality only dwell in the realm of the temporary; nothing that they have is really theirs. The very energy that sustains them, the Life Force (Prana) has been given by the Creator. The personality is merely that part of the inner you that you exhibit to the outer world. In many ways, it displays the degree to which you have evolved, for if the personality is warm, responsive, generous in thought and action to others, that is where you are on the ladder of your individual spiritual progress. Oh, there are those whose exterior personality is but a facade, but how many people can really possess a personality which indicates one way of life and an inner force which exemplifies another? Very few people are that versatile.

There is a great Cosmic Law which states, "What you think and feel you bring into form." This accounts for the conditions that exist in your life, for by the emplacement of your consciousness and your attention, you create, and your creations are but the reflection of what you thought and felt: "As above, so below", the microcosm reflecting the macrocosm. As you *are* a creator, (macrocosm), it follows that what you create (microcosm), will be qualified by and contain the characteristics of what is within you at the moment of thinking and feeling.

Another phase of this Truth states that where your thought is, there you are also. You are your consciousness, and what you think about, you become. If your thoughts and consciousness dwell upon hatreds, fears, jealousies, selfishness, etc., you reflect this externally. People sense these things in you through your vibrations, for thoughts are energy, and you send this out into the atmosphere around you.

Your character, your personality, respond to the quality of your thoughts, and this manifests in your dealings with others and in what your fellow man sees in you. Your reactions to situations in daily life, the working world, social, and home life, will correspond to the level of the thoughts you have been engaged in during each day. So, the Law of Responsibility then makes you responsible for whatever occurs in your living. By the proper use of discrimination, attention, and consciousness, you can recognize where you are, what you are, and what you should be doing in your own life and in the lives of others.

Discord in your life results from your failure in correct and right thinking. Permitting yourself to dwell upon the negative and destructive thoughts brings the disharmony, the failures, the dissatisfactions to you. Your attention to these discordant negativisms incorporate them into your life's experiences. Thus they become part of the vibrations which you emit, and your auric field depicts this and influences you and those with whom you come into contact. Following the Law of what you think, you become, your attention to negative thoughts gives energy and form to them, and they become actual entities which then have power to condition you and the life around you.

The Law of Individual Responsibility is most important, for by observing it, you learn to guard your thoughts and feelings. Feelings must be curbed carefully, for thoughts only assume form when clothed with feeling. Emotions or desires are the momentum behind the actualization of thought.

The Law continues once you have set into motion, for by what you think and feel, you attract—illness, disease, disintegration or success, happiness, health. Through transmuting your lower thoughts to a higher plane, you produce the constructive forces to convey the opposite polarity into your existence. You then witness the positive features of life. Instead of destroying your being with discord and disharmony by giving expression to negative thoughts, you should build a firm foundation for yourself. Unfortunate activities enter your sphere only as you permit them.

You might ask: How can I restrict my thoughts and feelings from the destructive forces about me? How might I condition myself to control thought and feeling and channel them into the constructive? This is where discipline enters—the goal of the yogis—self-discipline. You cannot, of course, attain this state without constant, conscious, and determined effort. Nothing is ever reached without this effort.

Nothing is impossible if you *will* it and try it. There are certain established procedures, time-tested over the centuries to prove that it can be done. The first thing you must do is to control and to quiet all activity of the body and the mind. Naturally, this is not easy and requires patience and time. You will succeed, fail, succeed—time and time again. Try to reach this quiet state by doing it every day for five to ten minutes. Stretch the time further if you so wish. There is no time limit to effort in this direction. Any time of the day will do, but if you set aside the morning before you engage in the daily routine affairs, you might be amazed at the results—not only of becoming quiet, but also in the changes that evidence themselves in your usual day. Things will go better!

Secondly, make sure that you will not be disturbed in this period when trying to become still. You cannot quiet yourself when all about you is confusion and chaos. Once you learn stillness, you can slip into that state regardless of noise around you, but that comes *after* you have learned *how* to become quiet and still. It is necessary to be alone and undisturbed so that you reduce the impingements on your mind. If you are subject to distractions of others moving about or talking, your body and mind become restless.

When you manage this stillness, imagine yourself surrounded by a white light. This light protects you while still and aids in stimulating the heart chakra (psychic center) which begins radiating and increasing the energy flow. The white light aids in improving your health while you sit quietly. In fact, the use of the white light is a focal point of attention in occult metaphysics; it is used for health, meditation, protection, etc.

I travel a great deal and before departing on any trip, I envision my automobile, surrounded by white light, leaving my home and arriving at its destination. I think of my car as never being a vehicle of destruction to human or animal life or to property. During all the years of traveling by car, it has never been a destructive instrument, and I have never been in an accident. My car has been damaged, but never while I was in it or while it was on the highways and in motion.

The metaphysical group which meets at my home on a regularly scheduled basis has used the white light for healing purposes.

The results have been most gratifying and very unusual. Of course, the group realizes that, in the long run, it does not matter if it was the white light that cured so long as the person improved. Still, we feel our use of the white light has been instrumental, for some cases were beyond hope; some were rather odd and in the realm of impossible to help, but in each case within a few hours after the white light treatment, improvement appeared.

So use the white light for yourself to assist yourself in becoming quiet and for protection.

Thirdly, knowledge and the recognition of the Higher Powers within you is necessary. Listen for that "still small voice within." With the awareness and recognition of the right, the Higher Powers assist you more strongly and clearly. See this Higher Power as permeating every cell in your body. Remember that every atom possesses its own individual intelligence, so the Higher Powers reside within each atom, each molecule, each cell in your body. The importance of this relates back to the statement made before—where your thought is, there you are.

Truth is universal and ever Truth. It has not altered any more than it was thousands of years ago. The white light that you call upon anywhere, anytime is as real as a flashlight or the electricity that you use in your homes. You need not rely upon what others declare is true in the employment of the white light, for all the proof needed for your satisfaction will come through the constant practice of it. All you need is the experience of its use and its workings. As in all things, basically, you are the real proof—you become it through practice.

Time to meditate should be made every day. Many of you pursue a full schedule and feel that time to meditate is a scarce item in your busy day. Review each of your days. How much idle time was spent in foolish pleasures? What minutes were stolen from the busy day to gossip over unimportant and unnecessary things? Have you spent precious, valuable time complaining about this or that or criticising what others do or say? Have you fretted or fumed about conditions in life or about things that have to be done?

Replace wasted, useless time in, at least, one period of meditation each twenty-four hours. There is nothing to lose except the foolish waste of good time, but much is gained. The Cosmic works through such media as the white light. All is possible through this, for the Law always works.

Many people state that they cannot do it, thereby creating their own limitations or self-created boundaries. Your attitude of mind is your stumbling block or preventative from achieving what you should. Perhaps your mental attitude fears or claims it cannot do what it terms is impossible. Again, nothing is impossible — your thinking only makes it so. Instead of conjuring up all sorts of excuses as to why you *cannot* do this in a meditation, why not figure out reasons why you *can* do it? Nothing is so difficult but that thinking makes it so.

Using the higher Forces within you changes everything in your environment and the outlook you have. The Higher Forces prove that everything is possible and you can scale the heights if you pay attention to the "voice within." Failing to be aware of and to recognize the Higher Self chains you. These chains are of your own forging, and you have to unbind the fetters of your mind and soul. No one can do this for you, for since you made the confining limitations, it must be you and you alone who breaks these limitations and frees the Higher Self to express in the mundane world. This expression of the Higher Self will make you master of your destiny. Mastership of self is primary.

In the Introduction, the Aquarian Age is mentioned — the New Age of which the young people today and metaphysical groups have long anticipated. It is the Renaissance of the modern world — another rebirth of knowledge and awareness. As the first Renaissance brought man out of the ignorance of the Dark Ages, this recent Renaissance ushers you, the present humanity, into a New Age of the Reality of Truth, the Truth which has been underlying all surface knowledge brought forth in other ages. The original Renaissance represented the revival or re-discovery of material truths and scientific advance, but the present Renaissance is the re-awakening of humanity to the Spiritual Truths, the underlying causes, the basis of all. Thus, polarity will be achieved as man balances the material, scientific knowledge with the spiritual.

As you tune in on the New Age and understand the Laws and Truths, you comprehend the conditions relevant to human life and experience. You learn that you can create and experience in the physical world, but you know that it all reflects *you*. The Law is meant for the propagation of all that is right and correct. Your *Will* could determine otherwise; the Law of Compensation brings you similar conditions that you have created and that you must suffer through until you decide, by the same *Will*, to transmute the energies.

Within every right and correct desire is the power of its fulfillment. Correct desires expand your life and express this expansion in the mundane phases of the worldly life. As you give substance and form to all you think, feel, and do, determine that what you think, feel, and do will be constructive. Your Higher Mind always strives for this positive end of the pole; you must force the outer or objective mind to guide itself into constructive channels. Thus, the Higher Mind and the objective mind become partners in your expansion.

The Creative Force or the Cosmic Root Substance is eternal in its essence. However, through the eons of time, you (man) have limited the expression of the Cosmic Root Substance in the physical plane and have even contributed an apparent perishability. Naturally, by adding these qualities, the very character of limitation and perishability or disintegration evidences itself in your life and the type of body you express through. Think of all the seeds (atoms, really) you have placed into the Cosmic Ether-seeds of distrust, hatred, fear, jealousy, anger, lust. Is it any wonder that the world conditions center in these very characteristics? Nature itself rebels and distributes its anger in natural catastrophes, qualified, of course, by geographic and climatic conditions.

You cannot conceive that you are responsible for the cataclysms which occur in nature, but it is so. So is war a product of you and the masses of mankind. You fill the atmosphere with all sorts of negativism and by the Law of Cause and Effect, Attraction, and Compensation, you (for you are the world), draw the unfortunate circumstances into your life and into the life of the world.

Nature, actually, moves on the principle of perfect balance. Imbalance is your creation through the thoughts, deeds, and feelings you harbor. Nature, then, offers an opportunity for all the negative to dissipate by producing effects in the form of storms, earthquakes, etc. In the original Creative Plan, such things were not meant to be, but you (mankind) created the situations (Causes) which led to Nature's acts (Effects).

Remember the Law of Responsibility. The storms and turmoils existing in your small world are yours and yours alone, but the individual storms in everyone's life add up to the world situations as you see them today. As your personal life is but a reflection of you, the world reflects *all of you* as a sum total of the entire world picture.

Regard, therefore, the four elements as a safety valve feature which permits the dissolvement of a force of negativism built up by humanity. Imagine the vortex of negative power which would exist in the ether if Nature did not assist. It could destory us all otherwise.

Each time you carry your negative thoughts against someone who is not of your race, religion, your station in life, you contribute to the force which Nature has to release in its own way. Whatever you emit enters the Great Sea of Universal Substance and returns to you, personally, and to the world in general. Those who engage in the "protest" movements today add to this situation. Violence only begets violence. Change is the Law of the Universe, and much can be gained if you work properly and constructively. Masses of shouting, screaming individuals who hurl insults and physically destory and harm others and property are as guilty of cosmic misdemeanor as is the guilt that these "protestors" feel belongs to the "establishment." Two wrongs never make a right, as the old saying goes, so those of you who revolt today, using the negative methods are as much in the wrong as those against whom you protest for the wrongs perpetrated in the past.

Imagine the Karma being amassed by the young college students who "sit-in," take over colleges, burn records, etc. How very strange that they proclaim "peace" and exhibit signs, posters, etc. on the theme, but they behave in such a manner that they are really disclaiming "peace." Love commands respect and harmony! Are those of you who say, "God is Love," "Love one another" really sincere? Look within yourself. Does every action (and reaction) that you display exemplify this, or is it merely a matter of giving "lip service" to these beliefs?

Knowingly or unknowingly, when you participate in movements which are violent and emotionally biased, you contribute to the negative force which Nature tries to mitigate — acting as a purifying agent. The ethers would be jammed with the contamination delivered there by the disruptive thoughts and feelings of humanity. Nature attempts to re-assert the purity or pristint atmosphere of the Cosmic by eliminating the dross of human emotions.

The Cosmic Root Substance is everywhere and at all times and available to all, but by your mental volition you qualify it. But how do you qualify it? This remains for you, the individual to determine as you analyze your thoughts and feelings.

Cosmic Law does not have to be accepted merely on Faith, for it is demonstrable. You must have Faith to apply it in your life in your thoughts and actions, and the Law then manifests in the physical. Draw your attention from the environment to the Inner Reality, for each transgression of the Law demands a penalty. All is governed by natural law and in cycles of reincarnation. You must accept the Law and harmonize yourself with it.

Everything in your life is a responsibility. You cannot allow the slightest task or obligation to be passed by or left undone, for it will

become an obstacle to your success. It is only when you display ignornace and stubbornness that you set the wheels in motion for
payment of misdeeds or neglected duties. Recognize the Law of
One and the Law of Harmony and thus fulfill all duties, accomplish
all tasks that come your way. This you can do if you would will it.

Hermes said, "The inner is like the outer; the lower like the
higher." This statement reflects you in where you are according to
the attentions you have in life, your state of awareness, your ap-
plications of the Cosmic Laws. The Law of Responsibility grants no
alibis for you, and you cannot compensate, in any way, for
weaknesses.

The Oneness that pervades the Universe is an external principle within self-conscious life. Comprehension and knowledge of
this Law are not exclusively the property of any one person or of
any specific group. All of you can possess this awareness and acceptance of the Law and express it to its fullness. Everything in the
manifested world is embued with the Law, but it remains for self-
conscious life to exert the *Will* or determination to express it and
along what path.

Once you identify yourself with the Absolute, the Cosmic
Substance, the All-Pervading Life, you become a self-conscious unit
focalized within the Supreme Intelligence. You become an intensified, individualized force of immortal Cosmic Substance, part of
It, yet always retaining your individuality within It. The mysteries of
life become unveilved to you.

Then, you are truly the "Captain of your Fate, the Master of
your Soul." When thus you arrrive, you are a vital, present example
of Truth, a blueprint for all others to follow. You express, by your
own election, these Truths in the mundane, physical life of form
and activity. It follows, also, that when having arrived at this stage,
it becomes mandatory that you help others.

Many make the mistake of withdrawing from the world, feeling
that by virtue of attainment, participation in material living is no
longer necessary. The responsibility of helping your brother is far
greater now than ever before. You *are* your brother's keeper (with
limitations). All who evolve must assist, by example and by all other
means, those lower on the scale of attainment in the human
kingdom and in all other kingdoms as well. So, do not expect to
escape bearing the burdens and problems of others; as you learn
the Laws and reflect them, you become a co-worker of the Cosmos
in giving a helping hand to others.

Again, you must approach even this with caution, for the Law
of Non-interference plays a dominant role. You can help others to

help themselves, but you cannot relieve them of the experiences of solving their problems in life. You might become overly enthusiastic in your state of successful achievement and extend yourself too far in desiring to share with others what you have learned.

You might ask, "If a person reaches this level, would he not know this when he helps others?" He should, but perfection is still not attained at this level. Even those of the Third Degree Initiation make mistakes. (This is one of the highest of the White Brotherhoods which is mentioned in a later chapter.) Adepts, avatars are not exempt from the common errors in helping too much. They, too, despite advanced status, err often, but their awareness and perspective is keener and the realization of error detected sooner and transmuted.

This also reminds us of the Law of De-Personalization. Do not expect so much of those who advance themselves spiritually. Remember that they, too, still learn on the higher levels. When you tend to idolize or to look with awe to a spiritually developed person, you invited trouble and disappointment. All idols have clay feet! Respect them for having scaled certain mountain tops, but reserve adoration for the Absolute. That alone is perfect, yet containing all the imperfections. All is in all.

Each and every one of you can decide to elevate yourself from all the limitations of the physical world at any time that you become willing to spend your efforts in that direction. The desire must be present and the effort made. So many of you seek all of this, but too often expect it to be handed to you. Nothing in the spiritual life is that easy—all requires work. If it is important to you, then you will try to attain it. Expending effort is really the test of the validity of your desire.

Recognition of the fact that you are the identical source from which all flows is basic to spiritual progress. Once you establish this recognition in your consciousness, you energize the Cosmic Root Substance within you to move within you and in your world. Your attention to this core of energy is the switch to the flow of Cosmic current. You thus release a flood of creative power.

The basis of all that is the sea of Cosmic Energy and it exists within you. You must make self-conscious effort to recognize, to be aware of, and to accept this, thus bringing understanding of the energy. Through it you express the Creative Force to a high degree of fulfillment, bringing spiritual evolvement and eradicating the discord in your life. The outer then mirrors the inner and is a pattern for others to see and to follow.

The Law of One pervades all throughout Eternity. Attention to this Cosmic Law aligns you with every member of all the kingdoms throughout all the Universes. Differences, prejudices once held, and misconceptions now fall away from you as your perspective encompasses all that was, is or shall be. The interrelationship of everything in the created world clearly demonstrates itself to you, and the purpose of all like is known.

There comes a tremendous relief within when this concept of Oneness is yours. So much of the puzzlement of life—the events of living, the why of people, places, things, the reasons for all of life—are clearer and acceptable. A calmness suffuses your entire body and mind. You view life, people, events with a different outlook and know that all that happens is meant to be, that everyone is where he has placed himself according to the Law of Cause and Effect. No longer will you despair for yourself or others in times of crisis, illness, death, for all is *one*; all serves.

You forget the former small annoyances in life. Possessions no longer are obsessions with you, for you realize that they can corrode a man's soul.

You must first recognize the Law of Duality that underlies creation. The physical is tangible; the Spiritual is not but is more real than the physical, which is temporary. Cosmic Law teaches you that the mind and soul are not the body but are Higher Forces working through the body.

God is dual, being both darkness and light, positive and negative. This principle of the duality of the Absolute is best expressed in the Yang and Yin theory of opposites, which stresses the balancing of the opposite ends of the pole.

Truth is only attained by you in an ascending spiral, the apex of which resides in the "heart"—the spiritual heart and not the physical one. To ascend to the Truth, there must be a devotion to the Truth and your *effort to be* and *to become*. Actually, Truth will arrive as you learn and experience, for the unworthy person does not glimpse the Truth and the ONE.

Learn the crucible of Nature. Learn to be independent in life and to remain within the scope of purpose of your incarnation. Be honest and fair in your dealings with others and with yourself as well. Also, service should be a strong characteristic of your make-up.

Everything within Nature is within you, who embody all the elements. With Nature's elements and Laws, you can create and build forces and energies which will result in either good or evil for you.

Both God and Nature bestow their energies to you as an incarnate soul. Entrusted to you are all their forces and powers of the Realm of God, but they must be employed by you for right use. Primarily, *all* is meant for everyone to enjoy, but often selfishness appears, and you use the Cosmic Energy for personal gratification or ego-centered adoration. You must use all for the good of all, or you invite devastating circumstances in your life.

All of the Cosmos is related to and reproduced within you. If you refuse to work with the Cosmic or to unfold these latent forces you possess and live only from the outer awareness, you retard your spiritual progress. Indulgence in the attentions of the lower animal life brings impermanent and temporary satisfactions.

You must always be a reflection of the World Mind, despite the apparent limitations imposed upon you by personality, world events, etc. In every aspect of your environment, radiate the attributes of the Divine. Thus others will learn to lift themselves out of their self-created suffering and sorrow. Be a pulsating microcosm in harmony with the Macrocosm.

Throughout modern ages, science has condemned the ancient alchemists, little realizing that present-day science is unaware of what the alchemists sought. Misconceptions arose through misknowledge. The ancient ones were concentrating on the One-ness of life. If there is the One-ness, then, the alchemists reasoned, man can possess the Higher Forces of creation. Their direction was spiritual but their use of the physical elements and compounds confused scientists. "As above, so below" and "All is in all" were the basis of their efforts, for if all *is* in all, then all is subject to a transmutation (really a redemption). Man is not meant to be a slave to the physical appurtenances of life, but through the experience of the dense matter of life, he is supposed to elevate, to transmute *all* that is to a higher, spiritual plane.

The underlying Truth behind alchemy is the upliftment of the baser elements within you to the more spiritual.

In you a personal alchemy takes place as you evolve and unfold the God qualities you possess. Through sheer *Will*, you must overcome the personal self, spiritualize the atoms and the cells of your body, purify your senses. When you become aware of the Oneness of the Cosmic and become at-one-ment with the Creator, you gain dominion over yourself and over all other kingdoms. Spiritual alchemy accelerates evolution. It is a transcendental experience for you, a personal experience of the proof of the Oneness of the Cosmic Plan.

This spiritual alchemy cannot be yours without effort. Growth results from effort. You can easily fail if you do not learn that you have to give up things—you must often sacrifice. But if you do these things, you generate a force which then aids you in your transmutation. "As ye sow, so shall ye reap."

How many of you read about this subject in the available literature? How many of you sit at the feet of a guru or listen to authoritative lectures on these principles? Yet how many of those who do read, go to lectures, join groups, etc. make a real effort? If asked to give up money, time, place themselves at the disposal of the Cosmic to ". . .do their Father's work", how many would abandon their world of physical pleasures and comfort? How many will attempt to bridge the gap between the Higher Self and the lower self and indicate that the soul comprehends the Cosmic Laws and realizes the Oneness of all?

To transmute yourself, you must study the Laws, apply them in every day living. Put them into practice on a practical level—at home, at work, or at play. Then you and all those around you will see that the Cosmic Laws are capable of being demonstrated.

Spiritual growth or transmutation is a Holy Arcanum and through this achievement, you unveil the Mystery of life. The "ascension" was not only a spiritual one, but a physical transmutation as well.

Realize that there is but the Cosmic which is the world and manifests through all of the world's varied forms. It is the Over-Soul of the Universe, and you are the "word made flesh," the microscopic reflection. Have the Faith in this power and you can transmute anything in your nature to the purity of the Spirit (God.).

Are you one to scale the mountain tops or will you be content to dwell at the base of the mountain? Which attracts you more?

The Law of Life is the Will of God. There is no entrance through any "gates" to spirituality until you learn that you must obey the Cosmic Laws and the "still, small voice within." Attune yourself to the Law of Life and all you seek of the mystery of life will be offered to you.

The general conditions in your life and the planetary conditions today are a result of selfishness the individual and the mass awareness of the environment created. Most of you are painfully aware of the disastrous conditions surrounding you and the earth. This is becoming a common awareness, and man is seeking the means whereby these unfortunate situations might be transmuted in constructive and spiritual forces. All lies within each of you to try to transmute through a spiritual alchemy.

The Cosmic bestows its powers rather lavishly upon you to use in your evolvement. These powers are, of course, to be used positively. However, the chaotic conditions you witness today seem to be a testimonial of man's misuse of these powers. Man's inhumanity to man adequately indicates that most of humanity does not seem ready to accept this force for unselfish reasons.

Most people do not realize that when the Cosmic Power is used for the good of all men, it then helps the individual. You work at the wrong end of the pole when you attempt to move to the Laws and Truths for yourself first. You are steeped in a bog of selfishness, and until you eradicate this, ;you will not be entrusted with all that the Cosmic has to offer you. When you, individually, advance through your own efforts and rid yourself of greed and envy, hate and prejudice, the Cosmic pours its energies into and around you for your benefit and the benefit of others.

The basic Law of Life is the Law of Harmony (Love). This Law is the regulating factor for every aspect of the manifested worlds. It pervades the daily life experiences; it is involved in scientific fields.

So long as you are a self-conscious individual with mind as an attribute, you should observe this Law. Non-recognition or non-obedience to this Truth could cause you to lose, eventually, even the physical. Anything existing that is not rooted in this principle, will have its form disintegrated. This is true regardless of whether it is a physical form or a thought form.

All of you should remember that you are creators in your own right and you are doing this continuously. Since you use the Cosmic Power, you have the ability within yourself to create constructively and, also, to transmute the negative creations—the intentional and the non-intentional ones. Your limitations exist only because of the fact that you have created negatively, so to free yourself, you must transmute or disintegrate the unconstructive. You are the weaver of the net of discord and chaos that surrounds you twenty-four hours a day. You manufacture these conditions, but also, you may discharge these patterns from your life by dwelling in and living from the soul center in your true being.

Harmony is the basic force behind the manifestation of all forms; without it there would be nothing. It is the unifying or cohesive energy of the universe which, also, could not exist without this Harmony. Even in the field of science, this principle maintains its power, for it represents the attraction between all forces in atomic and electronic structure.

Harmony, in the jargon of the common mind, could imply the

physical, material expression of love. In the occult Law, it is the attraction, the duality of all things that seek to unite themselves. Since even physical love signifies unification of two opposites in the mundane world, it would represent the principle of Harmony. Unfortunately, mankind has fallen away from the original implications of the Law and concentrates solely upon the physical, animal senses.

With proper perspective, you can see the Law of Harmony as being the basic ideal behind the manifested creations. Through the influence of the Law, direction is assumed by all that is and purpose as well. It is the energy that maintains motion and activity in *being* and it is the essence of *Prana*, the life breath.

Everything is usually portrayed in a vortex (of Cosmic Energy). All forms of life swirl in this vortex and, similar to the atom have a neucleus or a core (heart), and electrons spin around it. The core or seed center is the force of harmony and serves all forms in a manner comparable to the function of the magnetic pole to the earth. It is the cohesive, magnetic attraction that unifies all the parts to appear as a single unit.

Most of you observe the tangible forms of all existing within your area. How many of you think of each form as a mass of atoms, each individualistic and with its own intelligence? If you have, have you ever wondered what and why they remain so as to construct a visible form? Each atom whirls quite selectively and independently from every other atom. No single atom separates itself from another, yet retains its individuality.

The forms through which the Ultimate functions in the physical plane are just an aggragation of atoms, molecules, and cells, all with the above-mentioned qualities. Forms are the vehicles for the expression of Spirit in gross, dense matter. As the tangible forms serve in the physical plane, so are these forms serving on the higher planes but conditioned by the Laws governing those planes.

Granting all of this as a basic premise for life-forms on *all* planes, then you must discern that the forms are but temporary and that there exists a force, an energy, an intelligence behind it all. This is the Law of Harmony, Love, whatever you wish to term it. Without it, there is nothing—just unformed darkness of Universal Light. It could be the "nothing between" that Beckett mentions in her book, NETI-NETI; NOT THIS, NOT THAT.

This core, governed by the Law of Harmony, in occult circles, is the seed-atom of each individual. The seed-atom is that part of pure Spirit which created you and is you through all eternity. It remains throughout all your lifetimes—uncontaminated and perfect.

It sustains itself and cannot be destroyed. Actually, this is the immortality quality of each of you, and as you pass from incarnation to incarnation, you stamp upon it the developing soul-personality of yourself. It registers all that you have been and are. It is your record throughout all time. The Reality of Life, man's quest for the Golden Grail, is this true substance, from which all is created—The Eternal Life of the Absolute (God).

The Law of Harmony is the unifying principle behind the mystery of the atomic structure of life—the cohesive law in science. Without this Law, no attraction would exist and there would be no form. It sustains the dual characteristic of the Spirit by keeping the Law of Opposites functioning. Love, then, though misinterpreted, is the attraction which brings unity to everything and everyone—if properly used.

Through this Law of Harmony, the atoms form life; atoms are entities and represent the fulfillment of the statement, "The word is made flesh." Each atom represents a separate universe, but involved in all the universes much as our Universe, although independent from all the other galactic systems, is involved with all others.

Many years ago, I was much stimulated by a book by George Hunt Williamson, OTHER TONGUES, OTHER FLESH, for in the book he discussed our planetary system. The context encouraged my imagination, for I began to conceive of our Universe as 1) merely an atom in the structure of the Greater body of the Absolute. You and I, as humans, certainly are not that conscious of every atom within our respective bodies, but these atoms form the bodies we use. So, neither would the Absolute be *that* aware of every atom (Universe) which composes His Body. Yet as you and I are much concerned over our physical condition and attempt to care for it with proper food, rest, exercise, so does the Absolute care for His Body with food (Cosmic Law and Knowledge), rest (Cosmic Cycles), and exercise (Cosmic activity in spiritual descent and ascent.)

The ideas continued and I thought 2) that our Universe or galaxy is composed of a central sun (core or heart) surrounded by planets (electrons) which whirl in space, and as the atom, move rather independently, yet they do not separate from the over-all pattern. Since our planetary system has a sun and planets, could it not be (As above, so below) that the combined sun and planets are really a huge sun for a larger solar system? This, of course, could be carried on and on ad infinitum. This second idea pleased me, for it involved the oneness of the Creation and followed the Cosmic Laws, yet I am hesitant about it although, occultly, I can see the possibilities.

The Law of Harmony adequately indicates the mathematical precision with which the Creation was planned. Planets remain in their orbits, move with exacting speed, never collide. If there were no governing intelligence or plan, the Universe would be most chaotic.

In working with and through the Cosmic Laws, you have the strength to do anything—to scale the peaks, or if your *Will* so dictates, to sink into the mire of lower, animal-type living. For *you* decide the way of your life and thus invite the experiences commensurate with your decisions which place you in direct communication with the Higher Forces or involve you in the lower senses.

This Law must be mentioned so that you realize the extent of the responsibility of your *Will* and the type of life you choose to live. *You* cannot extinguish the Spirit, but the Soul, which is the individualized you, can be retarded to a great extent. So much so can this occur, and this might be difficult for you to believe, I know, but it happens—you can retard yourself *out of existence.* When any individual so wallows, life after life, in the animal or lower self that he sinks lower than the animals, the Spirit within withdraws. This action then causes all concerning you to cease.

After eons of time pass, that spark of Spirit that withdrew will again embardk upon physical life. It will carry the scars of experiences which you placed there, and you are once more involved in worldy living. However, you have caused much spiritual delay for yourself and have much Karma to work out.

Still, it is all yours to do. Nothing is every completely lost, and in the long run, you will progress.

It is the Absolute that give you life and form. The benefits derived can only be yours when you realize this and accept the knowledge that there is a GREAT PRESENCE within you and that you have the identical powers of this PRESENCE. Unless you do this, you will never utilize the forces or exhibit the God-qualities which are your heritage from the Father.

Dwelling solely on the principle of physical life results in pain and misery, but when you live within the Laws and Truths, your life results in happiness and success. The external things of the physical world are but temporary and are never really yours while on the material plane, for they belong to the Cosmic Root Substance.

Duality seeps into all phases of life. As you receive, you must give, for balance must be retained through the Universe and your particular, personal Universe. You must learn to serve to the best of your ability in the Cosmic Pattern of your incarnations.

Do not stand in judgment of others, but look only for the good that is in all. God is manifested in everything, so observe the facets of God-qualities that show themselves in all activities — even in what apparently are not good activities.

The outer appearance of you must display Harmony to life and to everything in that life as the inner you develops and becomes aware. You show this Harmony when you are at peace within. By attending to this feeling, you pour out Harmony to all and to everything, and your life becomes an example for all.

Attention and application of this Law of Harmony will lift you from the depths of despair, failure, illness, and bring the success, peace and happiness you seek.

COSMIC INFLUENCE

Within each of you is a power that has never been fully realized or used by you. It is the identical force or power behind the movement of the world, the pulse of the universe, for everything that manifests is energy and energy is motion. This same power governs all the universes, all the galaxies. If you would but tune in on this fantastic, unused power within you, you would find that your life, in its entirety, would change. Each of you possesses this limitless force and has great potential for spiritual development, and if you use this inner power, it could cure your illnesses, turn failure into success; joy would suffuse your entire being and bring order out of your chaotic world. This power can guide and direct you in all avenues of life, present new and interesting vistas of knowledge, assist you in your sorrows, guide you in locating solutions to your problems. It elevates you to a state of being in which happiness, liberation, and peace and harmony are yours.

This power is Cosmic Power, the essence of all that was, is, or ever will be — the Root Substance of creation. It can be yours for inspiration if you would but call upon it. However, you must desire it, seek it, for it will not, of its own accord, display itself to you. If called upon, it is there, ready to help you to a greater life and higher spirituality. The Cosmic Supply is inexhaustible, ever-present, and without limitations. It brings to you a store-house of wisdom; infinite love, perfect peace and harmony, great joy, and intelligence.

When can you call upon this Universal Cosmic Power? Anytime, anywhere, for anything. All can be yours if you know how to ask for it. However, let me caution you now. Be sure that what you ask for, you really and truly want. It is written that you *can* have anything you want in life, but be prepared for the responsibilities of what you get.

Of course, effort must still be expended by you. You cannot lounge around and expect the Cosmic to serve all your wants and desires. This attitude makes of the Cosmic a "genii" type power, subject to your whims and caprices. It is not that available. Its force is not denied to you if you sincerely, and with good intentions, seek its use.

Want to change your job or go on that longed-for vacation? Do you want to improve your skills, move from your present location? Too often, you work on the problems or projects from without, little realizing that the solutions to problems and the methods for projects lie within you. The external is but the manifestation of the internal, the physical expression of the spiritual, the microcosm reflecting the macrocosm. As you observe and believe in the Law of "as above, so below", you then witness the cause of all created externals as being seated in the Higher Self.

Most of you still tend to pause at this, for it seems beyond reason that everything that exists must first dwell on higher realms or planes and in your higher selves. Remember that Pure Spirit descended through the Higher Planes before it expressed itself on the physical, the last plane, the plane of dense, gross matter. Therefore, *all* has to exist on the Higher Planes before becoming a physical manifestation.

Therefore, all that *is*, exists on the Higher Planes—a vast sea of creative energy. Have the faith, and it can all be yours when you are ready for it, when you seek it, and when you have earned it. Recall the words. "As ye sow, so shall ye reap." The Cosmic is rooted in reciprocity—action and reaction, cause and effect. Ghandhi once said, "Faith is nothing but a living, wide-awake awareness of God within."

Naturally, you wonder how can you attain to all of this? Success, in the long run, depends upon how much you approach this awareness, how firm or strong you are in your beliefs so that, at no time, will you hesitate or compromise with the Truth. So many of you live in a world of pretense—not really showing yourselves as you really are within.

Too many of you might feel that it is very complicated, too involved a path to follow. This is not so, for it is really quite simple and easy. Once you know the fundamental Laws and Truths of life, you will find that they are basic to everyday living. *You*, and only you, have made life a complicated experience by pretense, affectation, improper values, false goals (gods?). The right goals brought about by the proper emplacement of consciousness assist you in achieving success and minimizing failures, which are not so terrible, for they should be viewed as stepping stones to correct action.

The best advice anyone can give you is to re-evaluate yourself and your mental attitudes toward yourself, toward others, toward life. Do not harbor feelings of hatred, criticism, or self-pity, but rather dwell upon harmonious thoughts and feelings toward the entire universe, remembering that everything that exists has purpose, has potentiality, and is exactly where it is meant to be on the evolutionary scale. And—ALL IS ONE, AND ONE IS ALL. When you can do this, your life will be a more effective one now and in the future.

Few of you realize the truth behind the statement, "As a man thinketh in his heart, so he is." You are where your mind or attention is, and what circumstances or events enter into your life are a result of you and on one else. Your thoughts can make you ill or well, poor or wealthy, and unhappy or filled with joy. The nature of your habitual thinking, by the Law of Attraction, brings you what you have deserved.

Remember you *are* what you think—the sum total of all thoughts you harbor all day long—day in and day out. Your destiny, your fate rests upon the thought-forms you are constantly creating. True, it is easier to blame the events and circumstances in your life on people, family situation, race membership, etc., but upon careful evaluation, you can see that everything that comes your way—both the good and the not-so-good—is the result of your doing and thinking.

In Psalm 8, David brings to your attention the glory of the position that you hold as an integral part of the created universe. "When I consider Thy heavens, the work of Thy fingers, the moon and the stars, which Thou hast ordained; what is man that Thou art mindful of him? And the Son of man that Thous visitest him? For Thou hast made him a little lower than the angels and hast crowned him with glory and honor. Thou madest him to have dominion over the works of Thy hands; Thou hast put all things under his feet; all sheep, year, and the beasts of the field, the fowl of the air and the fish of the sea, and whatsoever passeth through the paths of the seas."

Through all of this, David refers to the inner qualities latent within each of you. There are no limitations to what you can accomplish. Men have scaled mountains, gone into outer space, landed on the moon, and are exploring the depths of the ocean. What one can do, all of you can do. In today's trends, man is beginning to probe the inner recesses of the mind and is gradually awakening to the fact that he is his own Universe—a reflection of the greater Universe or Universes.

Limitations are but self-imposed when you think in terms of *not* being able to do this or to do that. In reality, there are no boundaries to the areas in which you can move and accomplish. History is replete with examples of those who refused to recognize, but more important, refused to *accept* limitations or obstacles. Of course, you realize that their success or failures were due largely to the motives behind their actions.

Many metaphysical groups emphasize that there should be a lack of attention paid to the self and to the ego. This can be readily understood if *too much* stress is placed on the ego, yet you cannot ignore the ego or the self, for they are important. When you become aware of your true self, you pay it homage and respect as a functioning part of the living spark of Divinity within you. It is the Divine Essence which created you (descended into the physical plane of matter and form) and animates and sustains you. It is the life-force, the life-monad or principle within you.

This awareness of the Self has nothing to do with egotism or self-promotion along similar lines but represents a recognition and a respect for the Divine Powers within you and around you. Recall that you are the microcosmic reflection of the Macrocosm, and as you respect, honor, and harmonize your Self, you not only respect, honor, and harmonize with the Dinve, but also with everything that manifests. How can you esteem others if you hold yourself in disrespect?

When you harbor weak and negative thoughts and attitudes about yourself, you cannot project constructive feelings towards those around you. The world is but the echo of what you carry within yourself in attitudes and thoughts about yourself.

So, remember that your Self, your Ego, are very important. They are the representation of the "inner" you, despite any external personality manifestations. Through your Self and your Ego, you can exhibit true spirituality.

Humanity, in general, tends to seek answers to problems through misdirection. Take the problem of peace. Can you legislate peace in marble halls or should it be accomplished within the hearts of each of you? Can the universe be understood by peering at it through telescopes and measuring it with divers machines, or can you better understand the enormity, complexity, and simplicity by looking first at yourself?

You are the universe. Again, "in the grain of sand is the universe." "As above, so below" is the Law involved here. Once you can fully comprehend yourself, you will comprehend the galactic systems.

There is no need to look *outside* of yourself to locate the answers to all things; all is within. Shakespeare said, "What a piece of work is man! How noble in reason, how infinite in faculty! In form and moving, how express and admirable! In action, how like an angel; in apprehension, how like a god."

Infinite intelligence is within you. Emerson said, "There is one mind common to all individual men and every man is an inlet to the same and all of the same." Thus, you possess the ability and potential to use free will, to develop imagination, to function with the powers of the Infinite that are within you. The mind you use is the Mind of God. There is nothing in the universe that you cannot do or cannot become once you are aware that you have access to all the forces of the Absolute. This links you to all that has been, is and ever will be.

Your life and every aspect of your life can change if you change your thoughts and keep them that way. Through this change, you transform your life. The majority of the problems you face are because of improper attention, poor discrimination, and personality defects. Very few problems are the result of life, of environment, of heredity. You must find the right way to do things—everything from the minutest incident to major affairs. Have you ever reflected on your condition when you wake up in the morning? Are you moody, disgruntled, unable to talk to until you have had coffee or breakfast? Do you realize what a chain reaction of negativism you initiate by such behavior or attitudes?

Many years ago during World War II, a Major Paul F. Weber related a story to me which influenced me greatly. He had a shoe store in one of the northwestern or midwestern towns. One morning he arose rather in a bad mood, snapped at his wife and the children. He went to the office, criticized the sales people and was rude to a telephone operator. In the middle of the morning, he suddenly reflected on the chain of reactions for which he was responsible. His wife, in all probability, yelled at the children, was curt to salespeople at the grocery store, etc. The children, likewise, in the same frame of emotionalism, undoubtedly caused teachers and classmates unpleasant hours. The telephone operator would be curt with succeeding callers. The Major realized how in his negative behavior he had been the cause of much misery. From that moment on, he made it a rule that, regardless of how he really felt, he would get up with a smile and be pleasant to all. For him it worked, and I can believe it, for I never remember seeing him arrive at the office and not be smiling. He seemed to set the tone of the day for all of us. Every member of his department enjoyed working for him and we all produced. He was one of the finest men I ever had the pleasure of knowing and one who made a lasting impression upon me.

Have you the right of negatively condition the lives of those around you? To live properly, you must be aware of and live according to immutable and ever-lasting Cosmic Laws and Truths. Upon these Laws and Truths, you construct the foundation of your "home" in life. It reminds you of the Biblical analogy of the house built on sand and the house built on rock. Your "home" should be so located that its foundation is firmly rooted in the Infinite Intelligence that resides within you. The foundation begins to be securely constructed when all you do, all you think, and all you say stems from that intelligence. Once you achieve this, your environment, be it family, work, social life will change for the better; life will assume a more satisfying hue; your goals will be attained; fulfillment will be yours.

As all this transformation takes place in your environment, there will be an accompanying alteration in your personality and character. Emerson once stated that religions reflect the personality of God and, thus, all attributes of personality and character reside within the Absolute. This, too, perhaps explains the divergence in religions throughout the world as the personality of God must, surely, reflect itself in the geographic conditions, ethnic cultures, etc. Since God is Law and Law is God, this Law exists within you and can function through the expressing of your personality and character (which are Divine in essence.)

The moment you evidence the Divine Personality, you eliminate the negative elements of hatred, jealousy, anger, and fear, for you bring understanding to your daily experiences and relationships in all areas of life. Too, you can then recognize the limited, undeveloped personalities of others who have not, as yet, attained to this level of development. With this understanding, coupled with compassion, help can be rendered by you in helping them to help themselves. They are caught in the mesh of their own weaving of misery, suffering, deprivation. With understanding on your part, you assist them to advance along a path of improving their lives, and, at the same time, you attain to greater spiritual evolvement. The compassionate understanding that you offer to "crippled" personalities helps them to ward off or to handle the misery and suffering they attract to themselves by the very nature of their personalities. Apply the Golden Rule here. Do not appear superior to alcoholics, drug addicts, or anyone whose behavior deviates from what might be termed the normal pattern.

Your understanding and help could be the guiding hand to elevate someone to a higher degree of behavior and thinking. When you do this, you activate a three-fold response—in yourself, in the person whom you assist, and in all who are in contact with you.

The Cosmic Energy exists all the time. Whenever you need it—in times of despair or a crisis in your life—you can turn to it for guidance and assistance. Through this, you see that the material world, the externalized expression of Spirit, is not causative. Rather, it is the effect of causes set into motion in previous times. Remember, too, that the physical world is temporary and that "that, too, will pass."

The causative force behind all manifestation in your life is the sum total of your attitudes, your thoughts, your feelings. Conditions in the environment are but suggestive conditions; it remains for the exertion of your will to reject or to accept these conditions. By using Cosmic Mind Power, you can, actually, set forces into motion that will create the environment as *you* want it to be.

A short time ago, a public official had to attend a conference on a state level, for the community for which he worked was constructing a new public facility and was seeking federal funds to help finance the project. About one week before the meeting with the state committee, this official checked with six other communities which had recently received federal grants. He wanted to know or wanted to gain some insight into what the state committee might request. One question asked of all six of the other communities could pose a problem and be a stumbling block to the project.

The official every night for ten minutes meditated upon the meeting and pictured the entire questioning period, but without the one question which would present difficulties. This procedure was followed every night for one week prior to the meeting.

On the day of the meeting, the official, architect, and members of the town council appeared before the state committee. All questions asked of other previous applicants were asked—except, the *one* not desired.

You can, if the motive is right and unselfish, condition future events in your life. By using Cosmic Energy, you draw mental pictures of how you wish a situation to resolve itself, how even a social function can be successful, how a prospective employer will react to you. There is no area in life that will escape your control when you use this method.

Again, let me caution you that you cannot alter, completely, the pattern of Karma (cause and effect), but you can mitigate some of it by proper and constructive Mind Power. You must pay your just debts, but you can create the situations in your life that will ease the way to payment. Always preface anything you seek by the thought, "If it meant to be," and accept it if it comes or does not.

As you operate this law of using Cosmic Mind Power by creating mental images of how you wish things to be, you will discover or notice subtle changes taking place in your life. Life will become more orderly; you will attain a balance in values and perspective. Too, life for you will be marked by more progress and development; there will be fewer losses, better health, greater energy to accomplish.

Have you ever puzzled over the fact of miracles? Do miracles seem out-of-the-ordinary, beyond the realm of everyday possibilities? Miracles are miracles only because you do not understand the principles involved behind the manifestation. Once you know these principles, the miracles lose their position as such and become merely a demonstration of Cosmic Law and Truth. Actually, miracles substantiate natural law and are not a violation of the law.

Miracles are the manifestation of higher laws and principles generally unknown and unused by the majority of mankind. Just applying the Cosmic Influences in forming our thoughts and establishing patterns which result in changed conditions is an example of a miracle. Once you believe (and the Law of Belief is a Law of Life) that Cosmic Power is within you and can be used by you, and you demonstrate this, changes in personality, conditions, and character result. Great growth exhibits itself in a spiritual way.

All you have to do to prove miracles is to apply any of the Cosmic Energy in your daily life. The alterations that ensue will startle you until you realize that you have set causes into operation that return in manifestations.

It is the functioning of your subconscious Mind Power, working through the creative law that brings results to you, based on the thoughts and feelings you have entertained. Thus, the conditions around you, the circumstances of your everyday life are but a reflection of your habitual thinking and feeling. "As a man thinketh in his heart, so he is" and by the Law of Attraction brings everything to him in all areas of living.

As stated previously, there is a Cosmic Scheme or Pattern functioning at all times — call it a Plan of God if you so wish. Each of you is here to fulfill the pattern or to operate within the framework as best that you are able according to your level of evolvement. You must, first, know where you are on the evolutionary scale and learn to express the highest that is within you at that point. This, of course, depends mainly on the use of your feelings and your thoughts.

People, in general, lack direction in life. Are you guilty of this?

Do you wonder what to do next, when to do what you decide? You must realize that all you really have is the eternal "now." "Now" is the time to do things. No future can be determined unless the effort is made "now" where living and learning are concerned.

All that is has always been; you give form and expression and energy behind what exists on higher planes and bring it to physical and material manifestation.

Do not concern yourself with what will be. If you desire peace, peace is "now;" success is "now," not later. The future *is* "now" according to your efforts, yur sincerity, and your motives behind all this. When you worry about the future, you worry about something "now." When you involve yourself in dwelling on the past or in being fretful of the future, you rob yourself of the grandeur of the present. Forget the past and count your blessings where you are, considering your present status as the promise of tomorrow.

Shakespeare and the BIBLE remind us of the glories of the present "now."

It is "now" that you have the opportunities to learn, to experience, to grow. What has been and has finished cannot be undone. What *is* and will *be* depend upon what you are, where you are, and what you are doing about it "now." This is the all important factor. Even spirituality is unattainable in the future if you are not attending to it "now." Do not say, "I'll start that tomorrow." Today is the tomorrow you talked about yesterday.

The emphasis on the "now" not only applies to the spiritual and mental planes of life, but also to the material plane. Despite repetition, remember that you can have everything you wish in life; just be certain that what you desire is right and correct. Even if not right and correct, what you so desire can be yours, but it will be qualified by the fact that the payment will be measured and alloted according to the quality of the desire and the motives behind the desire.

Cosmic Power stimulates, animates all the universes. This power is the Life of God and is your life as well. It is available for you to use, but how will you use it? Will you use it wisely and constructively or destructively? Your will, your attention, your discrimination will be the factors in choosing and deciding its use. By the Law of Attraction, where you place your attention or consciousness will bring you a similar harvest—"As ye sow, so shall ye reap."

The purpose of each and every one of you in life is to manifest, to unfold, and to develop the qualities, attributes, and potentials of the God within. This can be accomplished by each but not without trials and tribulations. However, these should not be viewed as negative, but rather as positive, for your pleasure should rest in overcoming the problems of life—challenges should be seen as stepping stones to development and not as deterrents to progress.

Use your power of thought, coupled with right and correct desire, for the Infinite Mind can be reached always; it is spaceless and timeless, belonging to the Eternal Now and Here. To use this available power requires that you move mentally from old habits and patterns of thought into a realm of thinking in which you concentrate on the manner in which things are as you wish them to be.

Change! The Law of Life is the Law of Change. When you are at work, do things differently—view your job and working associates in a more positive light. See life as a grand experiment. Alter your way of thinking—the subjects you discuss, the language you use.

Several years ago, a young man joined our group. He worked as a tree-man, cutting out diseased limbs and removing entire trees. It was outside work with rough associations. His attitudes toward his work and to his fellow workers were poor, and the language used was rather crude and frequently used. Within a year, the change in this person was astounding; he no longer viewed his employment in a negative way, but said that while in the trees he was closer to the heavens and to God. Incidently, when he first came to us, he believed in nothing, but had a strong desire to believe in *something* . Just a few months ago, in a conversatin, he resorted to an obscene phrase. I remarked at that point that he seemed to have dropped obscenity in his talk, and he stated, "I have no need for it now." His entire life has become a reflection of metaphysical seeking; he has finished high school and is now entertaining the idea of enrolling in college. He is married and has three children.

Remember that everything you think can become a reality—"The Word (thought) made flesh." These realities can then be embodied into life's experiences. But it remains for you to change the old patterns and to demonstrate what you believe in the many aspects of your daily life. It is up to you, as a free agent with free will, to do and to become what you will. No one is forcing you to be anything or to believe in anything. You must think and decide for yourself, for no one wants you to be reduced to an automaton.

The totality of life with its sufferings, pain, misery is a result of the abuse of Universal Cosmic Laws and Truths. The joys, the successes, the development in life are a result of the proper utilization of the Laws and Truths. Upon which is your attention?

Undoubtedly, some of you are questioning and are very skeptical of the fact that all of these forces and powers can be yours.

This attitude is essential and is a protection, for "fools rush in, etc." No one should venture, causally or merely intellectually, into the study of Cosmic Truth. Proceed with caution; believe in nothing that you do not understand. Any Law based on Truth will always work and manifest itself to you in life.

The pursuance of Cosmic Truth stresses, above all things, the individual responsiblity to life and to everything in that life. To choose and to decide are the greatest and the strongest quality that you possess. By so exercising this discriminative power (will) you demonstrate your own creative powers.

Do not feel that, for you, it is too late. It is never too late to follow the Cosmic Laws and to bring order and harmony to a disordered and inharmonious life. "Be still and know that I (you) am God." Always keep this particular statement before you and each step along the way will be easier and easier; decisions will be faster and firmer.

Again, none of this is really easy, but in the long run, the hard way *is* the easy way. If you have a problem or are struggling with decisions that must be made, follow this simple procedure: Find a quiet spot; relax and try to feel at peace; let your problem be placed before you and the Cosmic. Do not be emotionally upset during this. The answer *will* actually come, and you will *know* it and *recognize* it when it does. Then, you will make the right decision.

Actually, all is Thought. The universe is a mental one; you are a mental thought. Mental Law is the supreme Law and so it behooves each one of you to think rightly and correctly. Good thoughts result in good effects; evil thoughts produce evil. "By their fruits ye shall know them", for the seeds (thoughts) you plant will grow after their kind.

So, then, all of life is a result of mental laws (thoughts) at work. Thus the emphasis is placed on the individual responsibility of your thoughts. For your world is the net result of your thinking—past and present.

Have you ever stopped and asked yourself these questions: Where am I *now*? What am I thinking *now*? On what is my attention *now*? The reply to where you are and what you are lies in what you are mentally focused on *right now*! Where your attention, your feelings, and your desires are—that is where you are *now* and what you are *now*. Attention fixes your perceptive faculties on a definite object or subject, and it is most important in the acquisition of your knowledge. Attention is the key to the door of life.

Many of you might ask: Where does Faith enter into the picture? But what is Faith? Do you view it in reference to a definite creed or religious practice? Or is it something else, something deeper and truer than what is commonly accepted? Faith is a way of thinking—a belief in something, but too often, you confine the belief in antiquated ideas about the Supreme Force or the Cosmic—the old God of religions to whom each prays for something—the old God who distributes his favors by whim or caprice. Do you relegate the Absolute to a reproduction of humanity, possessing all the human frailties of jealousy, hatred, or vengeance?

Faith, in reality, should not be so much a matter of belief but more of what is true. Truth lies in the power or in the laws of your mind, which is the mind of the Universe. Once you know and realize the Cosmic Laws, apply them to everyday life and experience. The application represents a test of the validity of the Laws.

Through Faith in the Laws, you can be anything you wish to be, have anything that you so desire. As Ella Wilcox stated, "Thoughts are things. . .", and thus, what you think you attract, and often you become a reflection of your thoughts. Your entire life mirrors the thoughts you harbor, be they constructive or destructive. So it is that your life represents the composition of your thoughts patterns.

Faith is an essential facet of life; no one believes in nothing—not even the atheist although he professes non-belief. Belief in something—anything—is necessary to a full and richer life.

Most people profess Faith in a Divine Being or a Superior Force, but is this the criteria for True Faith? Faith is personal and is determined by the spiritual evolvement of the individual.

Have you ever evaluated or thought about *your* Faith? What is it? Let it be of great value—in things that are true and lasting. Believe in all that is good in life and in your fellow man. Believe that, eventually, all works out for the best. Know and the Cosmic Power is inexhaustible and is ever-present and available whenever you have need to call upon it. Vest your Faith in the permanent, not the impermanent. Physical material things do not last; they represent the external, the glamor of the world and are subject to change and deterioration.

The only real, permanent possession you have is Spirit and the Laws and Truths of Spirit. They are the Eternals. Have Faith in these and all else shall be given to you.

Realize that through faith your ideals, your desires, your goals can become actualities. It is through your Faith in the Laws and Truths that you are enabled to face present situations, to endure illnesses, to confront disappointments, to approach your fears, worries, and negative qualities and work to eliminate them. Faith gives you the courage to accomplish all of this. Shakespeare said, "Our doubts are traitors and make us lose the good we oft might win by fearing to attempt." By Faith and the application of the Cosmic Law, you can overcome all difficulties and surmount the challenges of life. But it is Faith and belief in that Faith, coupled with effort, that brings results. All you have to do is try it.

All things can be yours if you would exert yourself, think positively, and act constructively. Be firm in your Faith that it can be so and it will be. Cosmic or Root Substance constantly surrounds you and is, at all times, available to you if you would tap in on this source of all life and being.

Desire what you want, but always qualify your desire with the thought that it must be something you have earned or that "if it is meant to be." You'd be surprised how your desires become realizations and problems are solved.

A word or caution must be stated here, for you *can* have even those things you should not wish for or have not earned, for *all is possible*. However, in this you must be prepared to assume the responsibility and the payment (Cause and Effect). So it behooves you to seek only that which, through your discrimination, you know is right and correct.

About seven years ago, although satisfied with my home and environment, I suddenly felt a need to move in order that I might be able to have a location and facilities in which a metaphysical center would be established. First, I pondered over this thought. Did I really want to move? Was I ready to assume the responsibilities of a group undertaking? Was I prepared for it? After meditating, I felt that the move would be right and proper.

Using the Cosmic Principles, I sent out the thought of moving and the desire and need behind it. Sooner or later, the right place and the right home would present themselves. A few weeks later, I visited two ex-students of mine in order to prepare for their class reunion. I was in their home two hours and bought it that night. The home is exactly what I've always wanted, and it has fulfilled every need for the metaphysical group work.

Many times you desire much and attempt to bring your desires to fruition but meet with failure. Often, this failure leads to frustration, restlessness, dissatisfaction. These negative feelings result in unhappiness and illness. This does not have to be once you realize, as W.E. Henley so aptly phrased it, "I am the Captain of my fate; I am the Master of my soul."

It is your thoughts and emotions (feelings) which determine your destiny. However, it is because you place great important to the realization of desires that brings disaster, for not all of you are ready or are willing to accept the fact that perhaps what you desire is not necessary for your development, your growth, your experiences. One of the first great lessons I learned is to accept that maybe I am not meant to have certain things I desire, not meant to do certain things in life. These things could possibly not be so essential as I feel they are; they could even deter my growth.

Remember that the Cosmic Pattern of your life slowly and certainly works at all times. You can interfere—to a point—by your own desires and will power, but if your desires and will might disrupt the Pattern to a great degree, the Cosmic could step in and prevent this. It sounds rather paradoxical, does it not? Yet, it is logical from the viewpoint of Cosmic Knowledge. The Cosmic knows how much you can handle, what is necessary for your growth and development, and what you need in each life cycle. So, although you can have what you want and desire, be prepared to accept the workings of the Cosmic Laws as conditioning factors.

This acceptance on your part prevents frustration and disappointments. Now, it does not make of you a passive, mechanical person tied to the wheel of circumstances, for your will and desires, your discriminative faculties still form many and most of the environmental conditions in your life. Too, the Cosmic Law of Balance and Polarity ascertains that the cycle of life and its attending circumstances run parallel to the level of your state of development in any given incarnation. You will discover that rarely does a person meet the situations and circumstances beyond the plane of existence on which he is.

What you are habitually thinking and doing *now* is your future. So if you wish the future to be happy, peaceful, successful look within yourself and determine what thoughts you have been entertaining. Editoralize your thinking—honestly and sincerely—and you can project your future life before you.

Our present is but the sum total of all our yesterdays' thoughts and is the promise of tomorrow.

Do not accept yourself as something less than what you are. Be not satisfied with mediocrity as your place in life. The rivers of your mind and imagery can be changed and alter the complexion of your life. Obstacles are but challenges along the way. The totality of creation lies within you and is yours for the asking and the doing—but do it right, think it right, believe in the right.

Do not stand still in life—always grow, for it is the underlying Cosmic Principle. To stand still indicates stagnation and crystallization. The Cosmic is energy; energy implies motion. Motion is universal and constant, and so must be your growth.

Only as you grow can the Cosmic also expand, for it, too, remains a part of the ever-expanding universe. Alice Bailey in her AUTOBIOGRAPHY declared that since we are all part of the Cosmic Substance (God) and we are growing and expanding, so too is God. God is not a Crystallized Being but an ever-growing, ever-expanding Intellect and Force.

When you grow and develop, you transcend all the obstacles, the trials and tribulations of life. In order to attain this growth, you must become aware of the Cosmic Power latent within you, and in so doing, accept that the circumstances around you are of your own making and responsibility. Then, and only then, will you take the first step toward controlling life.

Again, it resolves itself to the matter of attention, the proper emplacement of consciousness. Where you mind or attention is, there you are. If you concentrate on the negative, on trouble, or on the aggragavations around you, you add fuel to the firs, so to speak. In time, by too much attention, these negativisms gain control over you.

Through Cosmic Influence and the application of Cosmic Law, you gain the necessary tools and knowledge with which you fortify yourself to carry your problems. With this knowledge comes the perspective to see the good in all things—change, illness, success, failure, life, death. Generally, the majority you fear death, fear change, dread illness. Life itself often frightens you. But armed with Cosmic knowledge, you see all things in their proper place, realize the value of every experience (the good and the seemingly not-so-good), and life becomes an exciting experiment in learning for you.

Life is eternal and so are you, thus making you an immortal being. Since life and you are eternal, so are the problems in living. Then, there is no escape from the troubles that exist in your life. Knowing this, why not face them and solve them with the help of Cosmic Law? Only by so doing will you solve them.

Your present world is a kaleidoscope of the present thoughts, aspirations, ideas, and dreams that inhabit your mind, thus molding or fashioning your present and your future. As you change your thinking, *your* particular universe changes, creating success instead of failure, affluence for poverty, health for sickness, peace for disharmony. By proper attention and working with the Law, delays, obstacles, impediments to your life cease to be. But in all this, remember that it is the Eternal Now in which to begin, and by supplanting all the habitual negative thinking with the constructive, your entire life changes now and for the future. Your travel in the direction of your thoughts and images residing in your mind.

"Seek and ye shall find." No truer words were ever uttered. Search for Cosmic Law and Truth, and after finding them, live according to their principles. Only this way can you arrive at peace and balance, for the Cosmic is Absolute Peace and Harmony. By being aware of the Laws, by application through effort on your part, you can overcome all obstacles regardless of circumstances.

Most of you worry too much and extend this over a period of time, depleting yourself of energy and vitality and the will to accomplish. Worry distorts the perspective of a situation and causes you to concentrate on a few things to the exclusion of everything else. Often, you neglect important details or obligations due to this.

Worry finds its roots in fears—a negative force accepted by you in your mind. Employ Cosmic Principles to your problems, and negativism and fear dissipate. The majority of your fears are illusionary anyway.

Just recall that thoughts are powerful energies which vibrate and create worldly manifestations according to the degree of attention you give them. They create your destiny, your fate, so by carefully controlling your thoughts, you can produce events and experiences in your life which are positive and beneficial to you.

What you think, you create; your feelings attract similar qualities in your life. You, actually, become what you think and feel. You are the alpha and the omega, the beginning and the end, of everything in your individual manifested universe.

There is no one else to blame. The Cosmic is impersonal and favors no particular person. The universe is rooted in God's harmony and order. You must find your own way to this harmony and order, but do not expect to change the outer world—just yourself and in so doing, the outer world will become a reflection of you, the microcosmic reproduction of the macrocosm.

MAN'S POWER

As mentioned previously, the present root race (6th) of mankind now finds itself, officially, (August, 1953) in the Aquarian Age or the New Age. There is a subtle awareness of this especially among the youth of the world, who seem to respond to the increased vibratory rate of the cycle.

Being a member of today's world, you have the golden opportunity of availing yourself of the tremendous benefits of the age for spiritual evolvement. The existence of these benefits are the result of acceleration of the entire vibratory rate of the planet and the Universal Life Streams that inhabit the earth. More and more intensified Cosmic Power pours from the Planetary Logi (gods), for the new Root Race will develop the Mind within this Cosmic Cycle. By Mind, it is implied the Spiritual Mind.

Emphasis in this cycle for the Sixth Root Race of the Aquarian Age centers in the spiritual advance, with the Higher Mind correlated with spiritual understanding and knowledge. All that the Cosmic has to offer presents itself to you so that you might advance as a part of the Absolute into newer and higher spheres of spiritual manifestation. Remnants of the Fifth Root Race will continue to survive in the initial stages of the new Cosmic Cycle, but unless they increase their awareness or consciousness to the Higher Mind and the tempo of spirituality, they will be removed from the Life Stream of the Race. Pure intellectualism, the gift of the Fifth Root Race, has no place in the New Age thought and movement. Positive feeling and understanding tempers cold intellect, and the Law of Harmony accompanies this for all who desire to use it.

You have to find yourself in the New Age. So many of today's youth express this concept, for as the heirs to the past and the rulers of the future, they have felt the impingement of the raised vibrations. Their consciousness is ready and prepared for the advent of the New Age activities. Unfortunately, although present day youth's consciousness is ready, their attentions are misdirected.

Unless they learn to realign themselves with *correct* New Age thought, they could very well lose the very thing they stress as their goals. They are quite obviously sincere in their thinking and searching and this will benefit them when they head in the right direction.

Youth cries for freedom and change, which underlies the entire movement of this cycle. As Manly P. Hall stated in his book, MAN, GRAND SYMBOL OF THE UNIVERSE, the *life* within the *form* (the physical bodies, social structures of society, etc.) now needs *new* forms through which to express in the New Age. However, you must realize that you do not destroy the entire structure of what was and have nothing with which to replace it. Certain features of a worthwhile character carry over into the new, and the residue is then discarded.

New forms for the planetary life stream should be more refined, stronger in character, greater in scope and purpose. The horizons of the New Age will be limitless, yet very simple, for the foundation of the Age is Harmony (Love) and Spirituality.

You should gear yourselves to awakening the faculties of awareness — the transcendental quality of the real *you*. Reality in its truest sense appears through transcendental experiences, but these experiences must be attained through proper channels and correct methods.

Today, youth realizes the values and benefits of these transcendental experiences, but lacking the knowledge and right guidance, they resort to artificial means to reach this stage. Drugs, alcohol, trance, seances are the "in" things, but the ultimate effect in these experimentations will be disastrous for them. What they are doing will destroy what they sincerely seek, and as said before, youth today is sincere in this search.

As is true in all ages and in all movements, you have the false and negative forces that come into play. The self-styled gurus, mediums, and those who advocate drug producing transcendental methods are the enemies of the young people. The final result of all these methods will be the disintegration of the *true* methods (psychic centers) which would give youth what it seeks, needs, and deserves.

You are a member of several Life Streams — individual, racial, national, planetary, and inter-galactic (all is in all). The inter-galactic might startle you, but keep in mind the Oneness and the Greater-Body of the Absolute. You are *one* in every aspect, and the Absolute is not confined to just one galaxy but resides in all.

Think in terms of yourself as containing Higher Forces within you and that so long as they are in there, you are a physical expression of them although the degree to which you express them depends upon the application of these forces in your daily life. The more that you express and apply them, the more of the mystery of creation will be given to you. By the application of Higher Forces, you will see who and why you are in Truth.

Dreams lack substance, as do shadows. So long as you rely upon external, material things for progress, happiness, or success, you deal with the shadow-world — no substance, no permanence. Attention to these phases of living bring you frustrations, for they are subject to change and impermanence and are *not* in the realm of immortality.

Fix your sights on the Reality of life — the immortal, permanent Reality of the Absolute, Universal Mind, or Cosmos. Alter your limited concept of this Higher Being. Graduate Him from the ancient concepts promulgated by the organized religions to a higher realization. The ox-cart concepts of all of life and the Infinite must give way to the New Age precepts.

The Absolute is not confined, as of old, to a given space — "up there," seated on a throne, having a smile on His countenance, and dispensing His justice. The man-made image of God conflicts and disintegrates when opposed by the philosophy of the new Cosmic Cycle. The God of old was "outside" of you; the God of this Age is within each and every person and everything, for *all* is part of His "word made flesh." The word "flesh" does not necessarily relate to the flesh and bones of animal and man, but to the fact that Spirit, in the physical plane, is *clothed* in many forms.

Once you accept this tenet or new version of the Ultimate, you will find that you have a renewed Faith in the Absolute. At the age of 14, I had become a complete atheist and quite a bitter one. Having experienced orthodoxy in religion and not having found the answers that I sought, I rejected my religion and relegated the God-of-my-fathers to a "has-been" condition.

In a few years, I was exposed to the occult metaphysical studies, and through these studies, a new version of God entered by consciousness, a God that I could accept as part of all life and of me and I as part of Him. I conceived the grandeur of the Oneness and with it the logical reasons for all life and all being. Everyone and everything had its place in the pattern of worldly events, and all things occurred for a reason. The arrival at this stage of awareness renewed my individual Faith in God, and today, I possess a firmer belief, a wider understanding of the Ultimate.

As I did, so can you, but always keep in mind that the awareness and development is a personal, individual one. No one can do it for you—just yourself. Proof of all this can only be yours, for you, no one else.

Once you awaken your *Self* to this conscious state, you can become a co-worker with the Creator. This status is yours when you find *it* within yourself. Then as you work from this inner center, your life, the circumstances in it, and above all, *you* begin to change, and this change is always for the better. Remember though, studying the Laws, listening to the Truth only will not get you the desired results. Put them into practice everyday in every way, and you will notice the difference. "By their fruits ye shall know them."

The duality of life brings about an intercourse between the good and the not-so-good, and inter-play of opposing forces which represents the polarity that keeps the Cosmic balance. You constantly swing as a pendulum from one side to the other, between what is right and that which is wrong—the alternating ends of the pole. Your life resolves itself in the New Age to attempting to locate that balance, to unify the opposites so that you can operate as *one* unit, but with the attributes of all.

Generally, you swing to the wrong end of the pole from time to time when you apply Truths and concepts to life. This is very natural, for mistakes are a common denominator among mankind. The results which derive are because of the wrong use of the Cosmic Law. The *Bible* portrays this very well in the example of Mary Magdalene, the harlot. She represents the lower end of the polarity with its emphasis on the physical, animal senses. Yet, at the same time, it illustrates the redemption or the transmutation which can take place when awareness, through the Christ Consciousness, is acknowledged. The Christ Consciousness represents the other end of the polarity.

Your attention should be on the positive polarity of the Christ Consciousness, and that attention will be the energy that loosens the chains that bind you to your physical, material desires and assists you in breaking the habits of these desires. In focusing mind and feelings on the customary desires, you re-enact the symbol of the crucifixion. *You* crucify your Higher Self on the cross of matter, the lower self desires being the nails which bind the Higher Self to the limitations of the physical life. The true Christ Consciousness cannot suffer the pains of crucifixion, but your Higher Self does, for it strains against "the ties that bind." It seeks expression at its highest level but is barred by your attention to the earthly pleasures.

The symbol of "Passover," according to Kabbalists, is the transmutation of your worldly consciousness (attention) to a state of spirituality. This state of spirituality is the Promised Land which is held out as a reward for effort, sincerity, and steady application of the Cosmic Laws. In order to reach the shores of the Promised Land, you must re-awaken the Christ Consciousness which is encased within (the sepulchre) and you resurrect it. The sepulchre, too, may be considered the limiting factors of the tangible world. Roll away your stone of disbelief, habitual wrong doing and thinking, and awaken the Higher Self (Christ) within. As Mary Magdalene witnessed the ascension of Christ, so compel the lower, animal propensities to recognize the dominion of the Higher Self over all activities in life.

There should be no question as to whether or not you should do this, for to engage in the progress of the New Age with its concentration on Oneness and transcendental transmutation of the physical life, it will be a requirement for you. Do not, either, put it off, day by day, for time (Cosmic Time in this matter) is short. Decide to do it *now*, the eternal, ever-present now. After all, it is really all you have, you know. *Now* is the time clock for you to Will to do it.

You are in a basic stage of awareness or consciousness. Gradually, you will come to that state of full awareness — the "I am" which is so often mentioned in religious literature and in occult writings. The "I am" Presence is within each of you and is the Reality of God residing in all his creations. In the human kingdom, it is accompanied by Mind, the creative, spiritual Mind of the Absolute. Remember that this "I am" Mind is universal and unconditioned and is the true and only real channel of communication with the Higher Self. Through the recognition, awareness, and use of this Mind or "I am" Presence, you reach your salvation.

The Universal Mind brings light and understanding to your life and strips away your ignorance and dissolves all false concepts. You remain in a state of mental darkness and spiritual regression until you recognize this Truth. Not since the last great civilization of Atlantis has the knowledge of the mighty "I am" Presence ever come forth into the world as it is now. You have been given a portion of the Divine Life Stream and are the guardians of it. How are you using it, protecting it, and qualifying it?

Intellectual attainments are to be encouraged, but intellectual knowledge alone will not result in conscious immortality or individual soul consciousness. On the contrary, it is often the direct means preventing its possessor from following the more humble path which would lead to soul evolution.

When you get out of harmony with the Cosmic Laws, you become self-destructive and bring about your own dissolution by the act of remaining in a state of discord or out of harmony. This is the real meaning of sin. You have made life complex and now you must work out the hidden, latent potentialities of the soul.

The soul is neither spirit nor matter but is the relation between them. It acts as a mediator between the duality and is the middle link between the Ultimate and His form. The soul could be considered the Christ Principle, whether in nature or in God.

The realities of life are the soul-satisfying things. They can be the consciousness that knows and appreciates the simple fundamentals of kindness, understanding, compassion, and brotherly love. The problems and negativisms exist because you have made the complexities and the false values to life by your wrong approach.

Each of you has some major characteristic which requires transmutation. Some of you know what it is and are working at it. Others of you are working so potently and so furiously that all else is forgotten and are failing in other directions. Or you can be so depressed by the lack of perfection within yourself that you neglect all efforts toward spiritual consciousness and you are hurt or swamped by self-pity. This leads to loss of valuable time and personality exagerration and retards soul evolvement.

What you have been given by the Absolute as part of His Mind you must use constructively, but the choice is yours to make. The Universal Mind is dual in nature, as everything is, and operates everywhere at all times—on the physical plane and the higher planes also. As you evolve your consciousness and reach into the Mind awareness, you unite the opposite ends of the pole. The polarization results in your approach and achievement of the Christ Consciousness, "the child." As with you, so the Universes were created in like fashion—by the spiritual polarization of the duality principle.

The qualities of the Universe were the gift to you from the Father to His children, but you have to nurture these qualities, make them blossom forth, and develop them through experience and knowledge in the world of human affairs. They are permanent qualities in pristine quality unless you scar them by improper use or value. Free Will is the factor within you that makes the decision.

Essentially, you are the essence of Spirit. One of the seven bodies which you possess is the Spirit Body, which vibrates at a higher rate of vibration than any of the other six. It is an eternal body and remains with you through all your incarnations. This is the body through which you should function, but you need to awaken and operate the forces of the other six. These six bodies must become spiritualized by you in order that you may arrive, in a developed state, to the seventh or Spirit Body.

As you develop the inner powers that are yours, one by one, the other bodies oscillate and you manifest the qualities of each in your physical life. The full development of all these bodies and the application of the qualities of them in the tangible world are prerequisite for the awakening, by you, of your Spirit Body. Then, when you awaken the seventh one, you exhibit the powers and characteristics of that body here on earth and become like Christ in thought, feeling, and deed. "Even as I have done, so can ye also, and more."

You have the powers to utilize these inner forces to transform your life by changing your ways of thinking, doing, and feeling. The patterns which exist in your life are merely exteriorizations of your thoughts and what those thoughts have prescribed. Your Soul is directly related to the Supreme Intelligence but hemmed in by having to cope with your dominant habits of thought and emotion. At this very moment, you are experiencing what you think and believe.

The destiny of a nation, the destiny of the Universe are made by what individuals think and do. You and other individuals are attracted to and brought together by the nature of your thoughts. Thus, the old cliche, "You are judged by the company you keep" is not so far amiss.

The majority of your thoughts are, generally, opposed to Universal Law and Order.

Fortunately for all of you, the Cosmos is spaceless and timeless, for the world of Spirit has no beginning and no ending. Your transgressions might be obstacles to your growth, but there is ample time (incarnation after incarnation) to rearrange your thoughts and feelings and beliefs. This does not mean, however, that you should or could delay making the effort for evolvement, for each delay could bring eventual regression and the risk of repetition of problems and circumstances in your life in the "now" and in future lives.

"They wandered in the wilderness for forty years." Have you checked your thinking and feeling of late? Are you not wandering in a wilderness of chaos and confusion? Look closely at the quality of your thoughts and feelings, and then you will know why there is a lack of direction and a desperate need for order and constructive purpose.

Going back to the idea of the Promised Land—the state of spiritual awareness or consciousness—look for it within yourself, not on the outside or in a geographical location. Geographically, where would you look? The singular Universe you know is but a speck in the over-all immensity of creation. There are millions of galaxies (100,000,000 detected so far by astronomers), beyond conception. Your own individual universe is the Promised Land of spiritual fulfillment. Once there, you are all of the Universes and all the galaxies beyond number and beyond description.

Spiritual awareness will come to you when you are at peace with yourself, mentally and spiritually. How do you arrive at this state of awareness? First, you have to have developed your wisdom and understanding—on a spiritual level. This implies the proper use of *will* in deciding the type of thoughts you are and will have, the feelings you will entertain, the things you will act upon. Since all your experiences mirror your thoughts, it is then wiser to select the good rather than the wrong.

Your will determines what you will do; wisdom is the selective factor. Wisdom might show you how and what to do and to think, but it is your *Will* that sets it all into motion. Will, therefore, can be likened to electricity, the energy (which is all that electricity is) behind the light that shines.

Christ said, "Go to the Temple within." What sort of Temple have you built within yourself? Of what materials are its walls, ceilings, and floors made? Will the Temple you construct withstand the torments of daily life, the storms of emotions? How firm a foundation in Truth have you set this Temple upon? Your ideas, thoughts, emotions, actions will be the construction of your Temple. Build then on Truth and Law and Harmony, and you will develop as a spiritualized unit of the Absolute in this world and be a co-worker with the Creator.

Matter has no power of itself—only through Spirit. You, as a reflection of the Higher Forces, give matter its importance by the attention you pay to it. You energize the higher entity of matter through the use and power of thinking and thus place matter on a higher level as you *feel* it to be. False concepts of matter enthrone it and enslave the Soul. When you enslave the Soul, intelligence has, then, no constructive power, for the Soul is the energy behind the intellect. it is how you stimulate all things that decides how and where each will be.

What you need most is to re-evaluate yourself and redeem your spirituality. Your Higher Self cannot come into its own so long as you harbor wickedness in your mind. Harboring negativisms shuts the door to the spiritual aspects of your life. There can be no discharging of responsibility when you dwell on the lower side of the duality.

This is why you and all mankind live in a condition of dissatisfaction, restlessness, moodiness. You have lost the balance of life by being out-of-harmony with the Cosmic Laws, and so discord reigns supreme and uncontested in your lives. You will never regain the balance until you become more spiritualized, and then you discover the peace of mind, the serenity, the health, the happiness you have always wanted.

Without spirituality in your life, there exists only the fear of life, the fear of death, the fear of insecurity for you. You have the power within you to enhance this and to make your life a fearful, distasteful journey, or you can solve the problem of spirituality and become at peace in life. Enter into the ocean of Cosmic Root Substance and Consciousness (all within yourself). You do not have to go any further than that. The trials of life, the trivia which annoys you — all will disappear, or rather, be transmuted by your new state of awareness or consciousness.

Whenever you are in the midst of confusion and chaos, beleaguered by problems and situations almost beyond solution, enter into "a silence" and seek the Great Presence within you. "Be still and know" The answer is always right there for you, but you must reach in to the "I am Presence" and become at-one-ment with it.

Yoga systems aim at the development of disciplines as a way of truth and spirituality. Disciplines are necessary in life in order to accomplish, for nothing can be gained if disorder and confusion reign in life. You find a constant strain between the Higher Forces within you and in the Cosmic and the negative elements which co-exist with the Higher Forces. This clash between the two opposites indicates the need for a greater perspective, knowledge and understanding of the cosmic Laws and Truths, which would re-orientate you to the positive approach to the use of the Higher Forces. Disciplinary measures here involve continuity of effort in study, steady application of the knowledge accumulated, and a firm resolution to keep on the one path to Truth.

You should not permit confusion or conflict of ideals to enter your consciousness, for the inner conflict shows in the outer world and creates problems for you in living. Reasoning — not necessarily rationalization — will bring you the progress and advancement you seek.

Remove the negative thoughts which habitually occupy your mind, for as you are the one who permitted entrance, you are the one who can eject them from your being. Otherwise, these negative thoughts become an integral part of your make-up and more difficult to eradicate as time goes by.

Thoughts are things and can assume form in the material world or are the circumstances in your atmosphere. The form assumed relates directly to the type of thought emanated, so if the forms or circumstances, following the Cosmic Law of Attraction, are ugly and displeasing, remember that you created them. As you made them, you can unmake them if you so desire.

Too many of you complain about your life, but continue to wade through multitudinous thoughts of materialism and physical pleasures, self-pity, criticisms and hatreds. Stop complaining, for you put yourself and all the conditions where you and they are. There is no one else to blame except yourself. If you do not like what you are or where you are, do something about it—it is that simple. Do not look for escape hatches, for there are none. You might satisfy the outer personality and objective mind by the projection of blame, but the *inner you knows* and knows that it knows.

No one should even try to convince you that this is easy, for it is not, but the best things in life do not come easily. It requires hard work, sincerity, and steady application to know and to apply each Law, such as Attention, Discrimination, Order, Harmony, Responsibility. Yet, in the final analysis, you will find that the *hard* way *is* the easy way.

Occult teachings stress the Law, "Be active calmly and calmly active." How difficult this is! The rewards, though, are really tremendous and gratifying. By using this Law, you correctly stimulate forces which will assist you in helping yourself to a postive way of life, problems solved, spirituality progressing.

If you make the slightest effort to attune yourself to the Universal Mind or the Cosmic Consciousness, and coupled with sincerity and determination, you will reach the state of awareness which grants you the vision of the Cosmic. Powers. This, then becomes the basis from which all your future activity is launched in your dealings with life and with others.

The Universe is not a static, crystallized Universe with fixed, immutable Laws, for the Law of Change is the Law of the Cosmos. This extends, particularly, to the physical plane. What a defeatist frustrating experience all this would be if it could not be changed. Imagine that through all eternity that there would be poverty, sickness, prejudice, etc., and no opportunity to alter them or to escape from these conditions. Man would indeed sink into the depths of despair, and rightly so, if this were the truth.

Fortunately for you and mankind, the Universe is in a fluidic state and the Law of the Change underlies all activity. Without this

Law, no progress could ever be made by anyone. Previously, it was stated that Truth, as matter, is always becoming, indicating thereby that Truth, although basically firm and permanent, can change. However, with Finite Truth, it is not so much a matter of change as it is the *extension* or *expansion* of Truth through new experiences, new thought, new forms.

This will be most evident in the New Age and, especially, the young as they positively develop their awareness. Their choice of direction, goals, and sincerity will determine their success in attaining the world that they *claim* they want.

All can be different as you arrive at a state of awareness which brings into play the soul qualities within you. Have Faith in the overall Cosmic Scheme, and all improves. If your Faith wavers, read the 91st Psalm and renew your strength and refurbish your mind to the inevitable success of the Cosmic Truth.

As you reaffirm these Truths in yourself, you will have more confidence as you go along the way, for it becomes easier for you with each step that you take and succeed.

It will be made clearer to you in a later chapter about letting go of your problems. The Spiritual Law is to let the problem go. If you dwell too much on the situation, it remains with you, within your auric field. The Higher Forces cannot help you if you keep it to yourself. Just become peaceful, mediate, and send out your thoughts as to what you want and how you want it. Have Faith that it will be, and it will.

Your problem, as so many, rests in the fact that you entertain many doubts and you vacillate too frequently. Do not doubt that the Law works, for it does unfailingly. It might be wiser to ponder over the question as to whether or not you have the understanding and the wisdom to use the Spiritual Laws properly.

Reject negative thoughts and feelings which you allow to run riot in your mind. These prevent the harmony to demonstrate, and so you hold yourself in chains. The limitations that exist within your life are the results of the negativisms holding sway over you. The level of your consciousness is the quality of your thinking and feeling.

Every department of your life is colored by your views, your thoughts, your deeds. When you carry hatred or resentments, when you stand in judgment upon others, when you attend only to the outer shells that you see, it is only because these things are within you. These are the illusory features of life, the glamour to which you pay so much attention. Seek only the true and the real rather than the false and the temporary, and your life will become free of the limitations which you have placed on it.

Undoubtedly, you, as well as the masses of mankind, have fallen prey to misconceptions of Truth—especially that there is to be a final day of judgment. At that time, according to the myth, all will rise from the grave, and they and the living will face God. There is no such thing as *one* final day of judgment. Every day, you are judged (occultly), and every day can be a resurrection. Your individual record of each day enters the Akashic Record (sum total of all your deeds and thoughts through all incarnations), and the judgment is automatically passed right there and then, by the Cosmic Law and by *your* Higher Self. By virtue of the quality of your day, your future is conditioned by the record you *cause* to be enscribed in the Great Book.

This record holds for all time, and at the end of each incarnation, your soul meets the totality of its life—both the good and the not-so-good (called the Terror on the Threshhold). The soul's review of the immediate life-time is the experience depicted in the fable of the River Styx. The monsters and deformed creatures encountered on that crossing represent the wrong doings instigated during your sojourn in life. By firm Faith in the Cosmic Laws and Truths, the Soul can cross safely.

However, since few have reached perfection and all have committed some wrongs, every Soul has this to go through. With knowledge and understanding, the Soul could, at that time, mitigate some of the negative Karma that it accumulated by transmuting it.

Once you know that this will be part of your pattern or the continuity of consciousness after the so-called death, you can prepare for it. There is also an exercise, taught in ancient occult teachings, by which you can transmute each day, thereby easing the load for the Soul in the period immediately after death.

Try this. Each day, upon retiring, lie quietly and review your day, from the point at which you are at that moment to the very minute that you awakened in the morning. Call it a review in reverse, if you wish. Think deeply of how you treated others, of what you said, of what thoughts you allowed to reside in your mind, of your reactions to others. Were you guilty of criticism? Were you cross with anyone? What upset you during the day and how did you react to it? What hatreds, fears, anger occupied your emotions? Conversely, recognize, too, all the good things, but view them objectively, not in a self-centered attitude of pride.

All the negative can be transmuted; the energy can be redirected through the recognition that the negative was incorrect. Where you felt hatred for someone, bless them at once. Where fears existed, think and know that all will be well and have the Faith that it will be. Eradicate anger and send love or harmony to those against whom you had been disturbed.

This simple procedure will transmute the negative energy you expended on that day into something positive and good. Now, the sincerity behind this must be very evident. Please do not think that you can continue the next day, repeating the previous day's attitudes, and feel you can rectify them at night. You must be sincerely making the effort to correct these habitually wrong ways. Otherwise, the review at night will not have any effect.

So, you can help yourself and your Soul even on the planes which are higher or the other dimensions of living by what you accomplish now. Your spiritual progress accelerates when you know and practice this—with correct motives and steady application of the Laws.

Just keep in mind that God is omnipotent and omnipresent. The Cosmic Infinite surrounds you from the day of Creation through eternity. Thus, can there be a *day of judgment*, which in actuality, would characterize the Ultimate as Finite rather than Infinite? The occult law of all has been, is, and ever will be should give you the answer to this last question.

As part of Spirit, you are Infinite and eternal; as physical man, you are Finite and conditioned by degrees of it. It is the Finite consciousness of you that conceives of a final *day*, for as you limit your daily life's experiences, you limit all of your life or lives.

The Infinite or Eternal *you* knows that it evolves and evolves. According to how much you are permitted to know, there are the seven planes of life with many incarnations in each as is necessary for you to attain perfection on each individual plane. You have, literally, thousands of incarnations in the physical plane alone, and then, there are the lives on the other planes. Beyond that, you cannot know, for it is enough for mankind to realize the immensity and scope of the planes and the bodies he has now and will have.

The Hidden Knowledge beyond the seven planes will be yours when you have reached perfection on all levels and all planes.

Be content with developing in the "here" and the "now," for it is all that you can handle. Attempts to go beyond these planes could bring disastrous results.

It all sounds rather exhausting, but the vision of the immortality, the eternal you should be a satisfying awareness of the One and that it resides within you, and *you* are One with the Absolute.

"As the student is ready, the teacher appears" is an occult statement and Cosmic Law. But you realize, of course, that the teacher (a person, a group, or literature in some form) is but the type of teacher matching the level of your own development. They, too, reflect you and the degree to which you know and apply the Cosmic Truths. When working with someone or a group, do not expect that the teacher or group will shift the responsibility of you knowing, learning, and doing. This is your responsibility and yours alone. The instructing media is only a channel for you—nothing more than that.

"Truth is ever becoming." As you learn more and more, you will notice that newer doors open to you greater vistas of greater knowledge. It resembles a series of steps. Each step must be taken before you go on to the next one. There is no skipping of a single one. Higher Truths unfold with each progressive move forward. There is no limit, no ending to the knowledge that lies before you.

Knowledge, similar to your problems in living, will depend largely upon the efforts you make. None of it comes to you without the initial interest, desire, and attempt being started by you. It will not be pushed upon you until you are ready for it, and as you evolve, the inner forces stir and encourage you to seek the knowledge. Once you decide that this is what you want, the ways open up to you to solve your problems and to obtain the needed information.

The acquisition of the Cosmic Laws and Truths brings to your developing consciousness the awareness of being at-one-ment with the Ultimate. Both the visible world and the invisible worlds are but diversified experiences of the Absolute. At this stage, you know that "you and the Father are One." The all pervading oneness encompasses all kingdoms, interrelates all, and demonstrates the Law of Harmony, for the Absolute and you are ONE.

Arrival at this stage of awareness brings you the Light of Truth. Before this you dwelled in ignorance and darkness (mental). As in all things, the choice is yours to make—either to be enlightened or to remain unknowing throughout this lifetime. Only as you utilize the powers within you, will you become fully aware of your true nature and spiritual inheritance.

What really occurs is that you draw upon the God-qualities that live within you, and you are One with Cosmic Truth. No longer will God be something that exists"outside" of yourself and be pictured in the image of old, but now you and the Absolute unite through the indwelling Spirit which you bring to light. There are many ways in which you can do this, but the Law of Harmony and spirituality are the basic fundamentals. Devotion to Truth, sincerity of effort, and the motives behind all of these will give you the direction you need.

Any of these methods suffices to arouse the Higher Forces you possess. All of them create the completely spiritualized man. When completely spiritualized, inner peace is achieved—the Heaven of the BIBLE. However, the inner peace will reflect in your outer world, and Heaven *will be* the outer world as well as the inner. As you are an example or an expression of the Cosmic Laws and Truths, all your worlds express the identical state of being. For as you and the Absolute are One, you and your worlds are One, transmuted to the highest level of cosmic expression.

Cause and Effect are the motors in the machinery of the Creation. You engage the motor or energy which sets into operation the machinery. Your care and observation of the rules governing the motor and machinery, determine the success of the product issued forth.

When you know the value and the responsibility of the entire production and work according to the manual (Laws and Truths), all result for the good. Occultly, in recognizing that the ultimate good is within you, it releases you somewhat from the Cause and Effect principle. As you practice the Golden Rule, your surroundings respond to the Law of Harmony, and the dynamics of Cause and Effect decrease somewhat for you.

There are many analogies upon which much could be explained to you, but in the New Age, direct Truth is to be preferred and greater progress made through this way. The undiluted Truth can hurt, but you have the responsibility of all your life, with its errors and its successes, so it is better to seek the Truth in its essence rather than to clothe it in symbolic fables or myths.

All is to be made known to you in this age—with clarity and vision. The responsibility of what you learn and apply will be entirely yours, but so will be the rewards or the harvest of your planting.

The primary step for you is self-mastery. Only when you have conquered yourself can you reach into the Higher Planes of consciousness. The knowledge of Truth brings you to a recognition of the Cosmic Powers within you, and you thus become the "child." Receiving Truth sheds light on all of life and reveals to you the so-called "mysteries of life." It is when you remain in ignorance or darkness that you do not receive this light of knowledge. But when you *know* the Truth within you, you possess the information that will open the doors to all knowledge in all the universes.

So often occult metaphysics refers to the Christ within or the Christ principle. The story of the manger and the birth of THE CHRIST is the symbol of each person's awareness of the Great Presence within him. This Presence is the Cosmos and represents the faculty of the Cosmos resident in you. The discovery of this Presence grants you the opportunity to use the power that relates to it.

Now can any of you so discover this Presence? Of course you can, but only as you develop your awareness and sincerely seek and desire to *know* (preparing the manger). This desire must be an unselfish one, however. Those of you who selfishly desire it, will not recognize it even though it is constantly present. It is not available merely for the asking, but readily exhibits itself to you when you know enough, apply enough, and desire enough.

The Christ Consciousness or Christ Principle represents the idea of a Saviour, but not, as taught in orthodox religions, a physical, material person. Jesus became *the* Saviour as He rose to the heights of His inner powers and became a True Son of God.

Now, the next few statements could be shattering ones, possibly, for you if your views on religion are rigid and a bit narrow. The duality rested in Jesus Christ as it does in all things. There was Jesus, the physical, reincarnated man, and at a certain age, the Christ was born within Jesus. In other words, when Jesus, the man, was ready, the Christ Principle or Consciousness took over and predominated.

This idea does not, in any way, reduce the glory or the quality of Jesus, who had evolved spiritually to perfection. It remains, rather, as a testimony or symbol for all of you who so desire to attain (live up to) to a Christ-like life. Jesus Himself said, "Even as I have done, so can ye also, and more." The "and more" indicates that there are still greater powers and higher knowledge yet to be learned, but perhaps not for the physical plane of life. Learning for you will not cease once you have gained self-mastery and no longer need to reincarnate in the physical sphere. The learning process extends through all levels of all planes of consciousness.

This brings to mind a statement made quite frequently by those who study occult metaphysics and feel that they have learned so much. Within the past three years, four people have said to me, "This is my last incarnation; I shall no longer need this body again." I have always said that when a person opens his mouth and utters his thoughts, you know exactly where he really is on the ladder of evolution. Those who make such statements have many surprises in store for them. In each of the four cases, the daily experiences were indicative of the *lack* of real knowledge or awareness.

It is true that, eventually, each one of you should evolve to the degree that the physical body and the experiences involved will not be needed. However, at that step, your life will exemplify all the

Cosmic Laws and Truths, and you would not pass such remarks as not going to reincarnate again.

Returning again to the Christ Principle, it should be noted here that with Jesus, as with Confucius, Buddha, Zoroaster, etc., the idea or energy behind the appearance of an embodied Saviour depended upon the need or the readiness of the people for such a manifestation. Generally, though not always so standard, a Saviour appears every two thousand years (more or less) for the different ages. Each Saviour brings the tone or key-note for the age. Saviours appear in various sections of the world according to the necessity of the time, and the cultural development of the inhabitants. History indicates that the general movement of Saviours has been a "westward movement."

Rumors persist, and there seems to be some evidence, that a Saviour or "world leader" is presently embodied in the physical. Apparently, an Ascended Master descended from the Higher Planes and in Egypt in 1956, became embodied. According to occult metaphysics and the ancient prophecies, this World Leader will be known to the populace by 1980 or shortly thereafter. Take this for what it is worth to you and as you can accept or reject it. This World Leader, by the way, is supposed to represent the new Aquarian Age and establish the Oneness of all mankind—one religion, one way of life for all who wish to live it, accept it and believe in it.

The Christ Idea has been promulgated by the organized churches but emphasizes Christ as outside of each one of you. It has deteriorated into an idol worshipping practice without the full meaning of the Christ made known to you. The ox-cart idea of Jesus Christ seems to relegate Him to what "was." In the Aquarian Age, you will not need the outer saviour, for you will be able to learn how to reach the inner Christ Consciousness within your daily experiences. The Saviour of the New Age will be a channel through which all Cosmic Truth will come, and he will guide those who signify readiness, who desire it sincerely, who apply it correctly.

You no longer need the external attention of specific or singular physical replicas of the Cosmic Truth in the form of a *Saviour*, for you should be aware of the fact that Spirit is everywhere, in everything. You, everything, everywhere are literally "crammed with heaven." The Universes resound the "music of the spheres" to you if your ears are attuned to it and you evolve steadily forward. This is what occurred in the life of Jesus and He became THE CHRIST.

The Law of Harmony, remember, is the basis of all. To be Christ-like and to indicate this in all aspects of your life, you must be fully conscious of the principle of Harmony or Love. You can make the "word made flesh" every moment, every hour of your conscious life. Christ has said that you can do it, and if He could, so can you. The manifestation of Love and the Oneness could be reflected through you if you so desired. It remains for you to decide, to desire, to know. It is your responsibility and your choice to make. No one can make it for you.

There will be an accompanying humility of understanding when you are at-one-ment with the Ultimate. There will be no need to announce to others of your arrival to this level, for you will display the quality of spiritual leadership. Your goals will be the liberation of all men from the chains of physical, animal desires and not for self-promotion, comfort and security. This New Age has a few self-announced spiritual leaders who draw crowds, but lack the true humility and real knowledge of the Cosmos. Observe their lives and what they say (aside from lectures) and you will *know* where they are.

Spiritual leadership will de-emphasize personality. The ego-centered drives will be transmuted into unselfish works for all mankind. Simplicity of expression, kindness, Harmony will be the strong characteristics of every spiritual leader in this New Age.

Since you are part of the New Cosmic Cycle, you should discover the Christ Principle which should hold dominion over all. As each of you attains to the Cosmic Consciousness, you must express it everywhere, with everyone, every day. By attaining to this consciousness, you assist in preparing the theme and the drives for the New Age; you help to set the stage, in other words, for the period of time. All this is done within yourself as you reach into the heart center of your being.

Yours, individually, is the challenge *to be* and *to become* One with the Christ Principle. Heed the clarion call of the Soul to be One with Truth, which never dies, is never symbolized in just a few leaders or church organizations, but is ever-lasting and yours to have and to hold. Use this spiritual power for the good of all in all the kingdoms, for you are your brother's keeper of the inhabitants of human, animal, vegetable, and mineral kingdoms.

As each of you uses the Cosmic Power, more of its presents itself to you. This, naturally, depends upon how you use what comes to you. If used constructively, it flows endlessly into your awareness; if destructively employed, the flow does not stop flowing exactly, but you cut yourself off from it. This is what occurs with mediums and psychics who force information or interpret incorrectly, but continue to hold seances and to predict. It also explains the difference between white and black magic.

All of the occult work centers around energy, which on the

physical plane, is embodies in forms, but all is energy manifested. The energy itself is impersonal and impartial and contains the rudiments of great power which you qualify through the use of thought. Energy then directs itself according to what momentum or purpose you ascribe to it. Here is where you can differentiate between the white (positive) and black (negative) magic (phenomena of manifestation). The two aspects of energy simply operate according to the thought patterns established by you.

Actually, is there such a thing as white magic or black magic for that matter? The features of either one are assumed when the streams of creative energy are worked upon by the thought-mind strength of each individual.

Assumption of being a white or a black magician should be viewed with great skepticism, for there are very few of either in existence. How many individuals have reached the state of awareness where they can function in either area of conscious application of Cosmic Power?

There are those who work with the Cosmic Power constructively, and so are *considered* to be working with the White Forces or Brotherhood. And there are those who use Cosmic Power for selfish, negative, animalistic purposes. They regard themselves as advocates of Satan, leaders of black forces, the Black Brotherhood. Very few of present humanity have attained to either level despite avid claims of having done so, but they do align themselves with the energy streams according to the motives, desires and willpower. You have the choice to decide which end of the polarity attracts you more.

Each of you is a meeting place for the Cosmic Energy (Rays), and, thus, each of you could be a creative center if you so wish. Synthesize yourself with the Cosmic Power underlying all of the seven main rays, and you will understand the knowledge and the Power behind each one. It is the seven Cosmic Rays that give to humanity and to all kingdoms the complete areas for the expression of the manifested Absolute.

When you begin to stimulate the force field within you, you realize that the knowledge obtained for the New Age will require that you erase the incomplete and insufficient old beliefs you once had. This is very difficult, for change is never easy. You have built your present life around the old concepts and tenets and now have to dismiss them. Often, it might not be so much a matter of dismiss as much as a matter of re-arrangement. Truth lives in all things but, often, is distorted or misinterpreted. The New Age knowledge will be geared to the eventual adjustment of these distortions and misconceptions.

Successful combating the antiquated ideas permits the Inner Spirit to transmute you and your thoughts. Your central ideas will revolve around wisdom, harmony, order, detachment, etc. Through proper disciplines in using the positive ideas everyday, you can arrive at a state which prepares you for Initiation and Illumination.

Study each Cosmic Law and Truth carefully; analyze it for you as an individual and know where and how you can put it into practice. What is it for and what does it really mean? Then, live with it from a dedicated viewpoint. If you do this with each Cosmic Principle that unfolds to you, you will receive more, but each must be positively applied in constructive ways. By so doing, your life's problems, circumstances, and environment will improve, and you become the Son of the Father, for you will be doing "your Father's work."

It is all there within you in this contact with the Universal Mind, the Cosmos with its Laws and Truths. As Christ said, "Go to the Temple within," and you are the Temple where the only true Initiations and Illumination can take place. Here is the Cosmos, the Harmonic Center of Being, and as you become illumined, the Cosmic can express itself stronger and more clearly through you, the vessel of Cosmic Energy. As Christ was the Truth, the Way, the Light, so can you also be. Footprints in the sands of Time can be yours when you listen to the "inner voice" and follow its guidance.

You are a duplicate of the Cosmos, the Absolute, the Creator. You were not created less than the angels, who are the Elohim or co-workers of God, but you are equal with them in potential. The Cosmic Mind created all things from His pristine substance and embodied His creations with forms according to specific needs of all planes through which to operate. The Cosmic Ideation resulted in Spirit inhabiting material forms on the lowest plane—the physical, earth plane.

Since "In the beginning was the Word (sound) and the Word was with God (Cosmos)," know that you are the Word and One with God. Sound energy is one of the greatest forces you contain within yourself. Think of this each time you say something. Reconsider your words as you utter them, for you create as you speak. Do you speak in anger or in harmony? Do you utter phrases tinged with sacrasm or with kindness?

Notice reactions of people when you hear someone speak sharply or rudely. Entire countenances change with the tones of the voice, for the tones imply motive and intent. The "Music of the spheres" contains the gamut of all Cosmic Sound.

Occultly, it has been told that the huge stones of the Great Pyramids in Egypt were moved through the creative power of

sound. The inner priests of Egypt guarded the secret force involved
in mantras and used it sparingly and wisely. The proper use of
sound (and magnetism) could be the answer sought by certain
government agencies to enter the U.F.O. which crashed in the late
Forties or early Fifties and is in government hands! There are two
such U.F.O.'s in the world today, and neither has been entered, nor
does any technological skill known so much as mark or scratch the
metallic surface of these crafts. Deny it as they undoubtedly will
and have, the governments involved would do well to investigate
the occult principles of Sound and Magnetism.

The "grain of Mustard Seed" dwells within each of you and
within it is the complete Cosmic Pattern—the Alpha and the
Omega of all creation. It is all there, waiting for each of you to unfold its purpose and meaning and its potentials. Each segment of
the Cosmic Pattern or Scheme will be unfolded as you sincerely
seek it. As you have the "seed atom" of your incarnations seated in
your spiritual heart center, so is the "seed atom" of the Cosmos
planted in the Cosmic Energy that pours its essence into all
manifested life.

In living from the heart center through the Law of Harmony,
you fertilize the ground for the "seed atom" to grow and blossom
forth into your life and into the lives of those around you. Do not
concern yourself about whether or not those in your environment
are ready for it or not, for the influence of your example might
locate more possible fertile soil in the other person. By example,
you show the other person the way to Truth and to Light. Then, he
is, from then on, responsible for the degree of his own development
and awareness, much as you were responsible for yours. As you ger-
minate the essence of Cosmic Law and Truth, your life blooms in its
inner beauty to display the fragrance of harmony to all kingdoms.

All that was, is, or shall be is a result of Mind. Everything that
manifests has its origins in thought and is a product of a casual
energy. It is through this Mental Energy that creation initiated the
Cosmic Consciousness and external life force. Even you, as an individual, began as a germ of thought in the Creator's Mind—an impersonal and impartial thought, but a thought, nevertheless.

As the Creator thought and all began its motion of being, so
you can think and create, for the identical force is within you. The
old parable of the great oak tree that grew from the little acorn is a
good example. Take an acorn some day—or any seed for that matter—and contemplate over it. Looking at the acorn or seed, realize
how within the infinitesimal seed is the entire pattern of the tree or
the planet, complete with stems, leaves, blossoms. It can be a start-

ling feeling to think of the scope and greatness contained within the tiny seed. "In the grain of sand is the Universe."

Think, too, in carrying this thought further, of how you were once just a thought and are the external expression or ideation of the Creator. How vast the complexity resident within that original idea! How humble it should make you feel. *You are* all that was, is, or ever shall be. This should also bring a feeling of great pride to you. However, have humility without humbleness; have pride without being proud.

The Cosmic Pattern of all life is there within you, so work to evolve yourself to the awareness of the fullness of life that you possess. Pursuit of the good, the constructive, and the application of what you learn will allow this Cosmic Power to unfold in a manifestation in *your* life. Life is an individual matter for growth and unfoldment, and at the same time, is interrelated to all things, persons, and places.

You can become aware of yourself and of all Law and Truth, and as you do so, you spiritualize every atom, every molecule, every cell in your body. Harboring the negative thoughts only devastates your being and blocks your spiritual progress.

Each of you has to decide which path you will choose to tread, and "as a man thinketh, so he is" will reflect that path. Your views of people, places, and events are echoes of what is in your own being as you pay attention to them. You draw the diagram of your life, establish the tone of its quality according to the state or the level of your consciousness. Life can be a thing of beauty and harmony and peace, or it can be one of ugliness, unrest, disharmony. "As ye sow, so shall ye reap."

The unwise use of imaginative activity creates and gives the substance of Reality to false and negative concepts in your lives. When you continuously pay attention to hatreds, fears, lusts, resentments, jealousies, anger, sorrows, you give strength and power to these negative forces, and they, in turn, become entities which hold sway over you and affect your life and the lives of those concerned with you.

You, as all mankind seems to do, make false gods out of the things upon which you focus your attention. Some of you tend to worship the monetary phase of life, making money, security, "things" your goal and your god. Others of you seek the gratifications of physical life as the all-important facet of living. Still, some indulge and wallow in a life of alcohol or drugs. The last is an escape from the responsibility of what you are and what you are *not* doing with your existence.

As your attention rests itself on those temporal and temporary things, you help them to grow (as seeds), and they become magnified to the point where they are the dominant characteristics of your life. Actually, they have no reality of power other than what you give them by your attention. Also, you create the force behind them.

What you create, you can disintegrate or negate. Rectify the erroneous emplacement of your attention on the "false gods" in your life by using Cosmic Energy in a correct manner. Since Cosmic Law and Truth are always available and operating, you should comprehend them and use them positively. At the very moment that you decide to seek and to use these Laws constructively, the knowledge of them is obtainable. Once attained, however, it becomes your responsibility to use them for the betterment of all and to be dedicated to the application of the Laws to your own life.

Truth is universal and belongs to all for all time. Show your readiness for it and you will receive the instructions needed. The student always demonstrates to the teacher what he wants to know according to where he is in his development. Attunement or at-one-ment with the Cosmic presents itself as a possibility at every moment of your life. When you attune to the Cosmic, you then illustrate Law, Truth, and Harmony in your world and in all the worlds, and you eliminate the wrong concepts and destroy the "false gods."

At this very moment do it! There is always the Eternal Now to accomplish. Remember that what you allow to enter into your mind and how you feed this with feeling will reproduce itself in your world and in its own kind. It becomes a sort of dynamic equation in living, for you are a dynamo, a motor to which you give impetus by thought and feeling. Thoughts and feelings bring all into manifestation as did the Idea of God, plus the Law of Harmony, propel creation.

Harboring negative emotions and thoughts fills your life with self-imposed limitations. Eventually, habitual negative emotions reign over you, and you lose control and are bound by the chains of your own forging. These emotions go into action and manifest in the chaotic, disruptive influences surrounding you in your daily experiences.

Your awareness of Spiritual Truth and Law and knowing that these are within you should make you *know* that you have no choice but to develop yourself spiritually or you remain forever the slave of the mundane world. Individual spirituality must be achieved by you, especially if you are exposed to the Higher Forces within you and you realize that you are part of the Cosmic Root

Substance. Once you do all this, the Higher Forces within you take over and you will live from the heart center. All of the psychic centers will revolve and move and sensitize you more and more.

As the still, small voice within you urges and guides you, your response to it opens the gates to greater and higher Truth. It is all there waiting for you to turn the key, for the Universal Mind seeks more channels to serve as an outlet for Its Laws and Truths. It cares not who you are, what your background is, what social level you are on. The only aspect It respects is that you are ready in your spiritual evolvement and aware of the Higher Consciousness that is yours.

Listen to that still, small voice within you. It can bring you all that you have inwardly wanted and yearned for, all that you have sought through the ages. Be a vessel for Cosmic Truth and turn your countenance to the higher, brighter horizons of living. Shun the untruth and become One with the Cosmic Force hidden within. It is your free will that will make the choice. Let it be the wise one, constructive and uplifting.

Creation was a definite, conscious act on the part of the Creator, and in the Cosmic Power is contained all the qualities and characteristics of the Absolute, which expressed these qualities universally. In so far as anyone can know on this level of development, there was first the Creator, then the idea, then the manifestation of that idea—what we term as Cosmic Ideation made manifest.

Singularly, you possess this very force and when you become aware of it, you must demonstrate it in your environment. Your special world grants you opportunities to reflect your Cosmic Power at work. Once you do this, the Higher Forces, working as Cosmic Energy through its individualized unit (you), expresses its supremacy over all that is. It functions through all things and on all levels or planes of existence. So when you measure up to these inner powers, you function on all levels.

When out-of-step, so to speak, with the rhythm or pulse beat of the Universe, you are unable to work on any plane other than that of the physical with its restrictions and limitations. By developing the knowledge and the sensitivity to the Higher Powers, you cross the boundaries of your physical being and reach up into the higher spheres.

Everything in your conscious area is a creation by you. Realize this and learn the responsibility of what you have done. Do not try to avoid the fact that all is yours—the good and the negative. Regardless of what it is in your surroundings, it is all but a projection of what you thought, felt, or did, and these affect you and all within your sphere of influence.

The entire world conditions and the conditions of the many

Universes mirror the negative and ignorant activity of you and all the masses of people. Few of you realize how much you contribute to the misery of the present-day world but tend to feel you are the *victim* rather than the initiator of all that occurs. Think back on the role Nature plays as an escape hatch for accumulated negative and poisonous energies. This accumulation, remember, represents the sum total of you and all mankind in thinking in terms of hatred, prejudice, fear, anger, etc.

See that the only escape from it all is through self-mastery, and that the negative exists only in so far as you unwisely use the Cosmic Law. Through self-mastery, you develop your inner spiritual power and raise your vibratory rate and contribute to increasing the vibratory rate of the race and the planet.

Blame for your immediate circumstances cannot be projected to others. You tend to look askance at the behavior of others; yet how about the skeletons in your closet? Lack of advancement in position could be because of your attitudes toward your work and not because the boss favors someone else or places a relative ahead of you. Is your neighbor uncooperative and difficult to live next to? Do sales people treat you discourteously?

All of these are merely one of two things—either you invite this sort of thing into your life by your own attitudes and feelings, or they are the tests to measure your ability to live within the Laws despite others or situations. The Laws of Attraction and Detachment operate in these respective areas.

Just imagine how you can alter the atmosphere in the lives of others by how you present yourself. The next time a sales person seems sarcastic or discourteous, try a smile, a kind word, a flattering remark, a "thank you" said sincerely. Watch the reaction on the facial features of the clerk. They will soften and you could be theone to re-make that person's day, and others that follow you will meet a clerk whose attitudes might be more pleasant.

Of course, as you involve yourself in this type of presentation of the working of the Cosmic Laws, you will be subject to the confidences, the problems, and the troubles of the people. Once you are at-one, this is the natural response to you by others. At this stage, you know enough and can shoulder these confidences competently. Also, you know how to place yourself in a shield of protection so that none of the negative auric energies emanating from the troubled person will affect or mingle with yours. This shield (white light) is especially important to use when dealing with those who are physically or psychologically ill.

Identify yourself with the Higher Mind at all times when you work with people and their problems. Keep in mind the Law of Non-interference, for you can only help them to adjust their attitudes and thoughts and guide them in the proper use of right thinking, right feeling, right action. In the final analysis, the effort must be theirs, but you can contribute to assisting them to help themselves.

Your Higher Self is a prisoner of any and all your negative thoughts and emotions. It can never be free to express fully the powers it has until you refuse to live in the depths of your wrong activities.

Become aware of the inner forces and follow the Biblical statement, "Let the mind that was in Christ Jesus be in you." It is there, but are you letting it *be*? Be-ness implies activity and motion, but the Christ Mind in you is only latent Mind until you give it the stimulus, the impetus so that it "moves and breathes" within you and thus in your life's work.

As Christ was, so can you also be — a True Son of the Father. You are, basically, a spiritual being and a container of the creative energies. Develop yourself spiritually and change the direction of your thoughts and you prove the existence of all of this, first, to yourself, and secondly, to the rest of the world.

Raise your vibrations from the lower, animal sense rate to a higher level of participation in the Cosmic Scheme. This will bring you to greater manifestation (spiritually) in all fields of endeavor.

You were born to create but only when you have attained this self-mastery which brings control of your thoughts and your emotions. Self-mastery implies contact with, awareness of, and functioning through your Higher Self. The ancient Greek philosopher Socrates said, "Know thyself," and in so doing this, you *know* the Reality of you in Truth.

Self-mastery means self-criticism and recognition of the fact that you are the instigator of where you are and what you are — again emphasizing the all importance of responsibility to life. Few of you might be willing to accept that it is you who create mental patterns that bring into existence all the situations and environmental factors. The mental patterns are created through choice, for you and you alone permit them house-room in your mind.

In order to achieve Self-mastery, the first step you must take is to curb your thinking and feeling. Evaluate your thoughts and eradicate the negative ones that enter. Guide your thoughts along the right, the constructive approaches, and thus affect the path of your life and what is in it.

Life in its entirety exists through and by the One Mind, which is also your Mind. All is interrelated by the Reality of being One.

Your Mind creates continuously. Is it a life full of monstrosities? If so, they are the creatures of your own making, the effect of what you allowed to center in your mind. If you are striving for spiritual development, be discriminative in the ideas you have and learn to use your *will* to make the right decisions. Self-mastery here makes you creator in the harmonious manifestation or materialization of *your* Cosmic Pattern.

Self-mastery tells you who you are in the ever-present "now." Forget yesterday and look not at what tomorrow might bring. Do the best you can with what you have where you are—NOW!

APPLICATION OF
OCCULT PHILOSOPHY

The course of history is replete with events that have shattered the thinking of the times and drastically altered the design of society, its structures, its beliefs. The Fall of Rome brought down the curtain on knowledge and on centralized authority, on law and order. The Renaissance re-opened the gates of learning and renewed the cultural life for man and brought tremendous progress. The Protestant Reformation resulted in the great religious schisms and dissensions and brought new wars and persecution to the people.

In the modern age, the enthronement of science, machinery, and all aspects of technology caused the world to shrink in terms of communication and transportation. This, too, changed the daily living habits of the world's population.

All of these aforementioned events or conditions greatly affected man, but it remained for the present century to produce the most striking occurrence. When man successfully split the atom, he wrought the most significant and far-reaching changes to humanity.

Until the splitting of the atom, matter reigned supreme—inviolable and secure to the physical sense of man. Suddenly, the Atomic Age appeared, and matter no longer resided in its "ivory towers." Humanity then realized that what they once thought as the firm foundation of everything, was not secure in itself. The "sacred cow" of the ages was sacrificed on the alter of the nuclear throne. All of life, formerly present in matter, was placed in awkwardness, for beliefs, ways of living were rooted in the security of the tangible forms. The structures of all phases of society's organization were based on this "false god" of matter.

Despite this new knowledge and awareness which accompanied the splitting of the atom, many still adhered to the old ideas and old ways, refusing change and resisting progress of the New Age Thought. Actually, the Atomic Age heralded the Aquarian Age with its emphasis on Mind and Spirituality.

In the late 1960's, even the theory of the supremacy of the

atom disintegrated with the discovery of the nutrino, which is below the atom. Could this be the force or energy behind the atom and perhaps, resemble more closely the essence of Spirit? Scientists, however, are beginning to feel that there is even a force or energy below the nutrino. Are we approaching the basis of the Reality of life? It is a debatable question, but this Age will bring many surprises in the discoveries about life and the energizing factors underlying it all.

Materiality now is in a dubious position of vulnerability in so far as permanence is concerned. The material world, like idols, suddenly has clay feet, and all those who sat at those feet now flounder in confusion and indecision.

The Law of Change holds sway over the conditions of society's construction, and the past few years witnessed the assumption of authority by this Law. Now, more than ever before, you must come to the realization of the impermanence of the mundane world and its physical features. The phenomena of materiality cannot be the center of your thinking and your believing. You have to look for that power which is behind the manifestation of material things to establish your tenets and focus your attentions. Shifting to the attentions of the forces behind the material world could lead you to the Reality you seek, the Reality which will be the theme of the New Age — Spirit.

You formerly sought your standards and values in the appurtenances of the physical life, and today, you see that these are no longer valid standards or values. Where will you go from here? Your search for Truth will continue, but in what direction — where and how will you look?

Look higher; probe into the other levels or planes of life, for in these are the higher, real expressions of what is expressed temporarily on the physical. Just remember that the physical life is but a transitory materialization of what exists, in higher forms and in greater and purer substance, on higher levels.

Your way to Reality in the Piscean and other past Ages seemed securely fastened to money, to governments, securities, armed might. All these seem futile gestures on your part in the New Age philosophy and way of life, which will be established eventually whether you agree with it or not. Your non-participation in this will not deter the facets of the Aquarian Age from materializing and functioning, so it behooves you to join the dynamic movement forward.

Realize, as always, that there will be minor movements which will flourish and have their basis in selfish ego-centeredness. Use the Law of Discrimination and follow what is right and what is correct. Intuition and knowledge will be the guidelines for you.

It will not be easy—this finding of the Absolute, for you will have to investigate now the invisible, intangible worlds. Before, it was all so simple to see, hear, touch, taste, and smell the material substances of what you thought was Reality. Now, Reality will not be so tangible in the sense of concreteness, but more real and more permanent than the other could ever be.

Do not lose your way in this search in the present Cosmic Cycle, for you must remain in the mainstream of positive occult metaphysical thinking. Certain schools, gurus, mediums, and psychics could misguide you in the mystical approach. Refresh your mind in that the energy of life can be misused by improper direction by those who supply the momentum of creative energy into negative approaches and channels of thinking and feeling and doing.

Do not allow self-asserted mystics to fool you—and there are many of those. The field of occult metaphysics lends itself most readily, unfortunately, to fraud and chicanery by unscrupulous people.

Another common misconception on the part of those who term themselves mystics lies in the fact that they equate their ideas of self-withdrawal from the responsibilities of worldly living with true mysticism. In its essence, this denial of responsibility and the rejection of the physical life are signals of doubt for you, for the Law clearly states that you are Spirit inhabiting the world of matter. Spirit enhances itself through the experiences in life and how *you* handle your spiritual evolution.

I am often amused by the appearances of the so-called mystics in the present day search by man for Truth. So often, they ape the sincere humility of past masters and mouth spiritualistic theory and phrases to captivated audiences. Their humility disappears to the eye and conscience when they enter their Cadillacs or their private planes to return to their retreates (villas) or homes. To me they make mockery of the Great Ones whose lives were simple and true examples of living. I do not profess to be an authority on these mystics, but if I were to select the person most sincere, most humble, most learned, I should nominate Krishnamurti.

Years ago, we once knew one of the supposed mystics of India. He was termed an avatar, and people raved about him, his teachings (which were excellent by the way), and his simplicity. At that time, I was a novice in the field of metaphysics, but I wondered silently, why his simplicity always displayed itself in the very luxurious mansions and penthouses of wealthy, elderly women.

Play a cautious game in the area of mysticism and the leader you select to follow. Remember, too, that the teachings are more important than the man. The external man could be only the channel through which the Cosmic has chosen to work. Far be it for you or me to judge the wisdom of the Cosmic, for there is always a good reason behind each of Its activities.

Too often, mystics and mysticism itself degenerate into a form of idol worship on the part of those who gather around them or who pursue the study of mysticism. Symbology in metaphysics plays a prominent role in the teachings of Truth, but, in themselves, the symbols are *not* the Truth, but merely representative of the idea of Truth. They are referred to as the visual aids in metaphysical learning, but should not become the focal point of your attention.

Religions of old resorted to using symbols and to erecting idols or statues to exemplify the beliefs. In time, the Church and man ascribed Truth to the *example* and, often, lost the Reality behind them. In the application of Cosmic Laws and Truth to life, a symbol could give you the meaning or the understanding you need, but that is all. Many times, you will find that you can use the symbol in meditation as a beginning point for focusing concentration, and from there, you go into the full meditation. This use of the symbol could be the means in meditation of attracting the Truth behind the symbol in the completeness of understanding.

The application of metaphysical teachings should bring Reality to you, but how? Through devoted effort and knowledge, much is revealed — the revelation of the Laws and Truths of the Cosmos. As Truth is given to you, you will be able to identify yourself with all that is, for you can be at-one with the Source of Life. Then, your life, your very being is a realization of the Source and a Reality *with* the Ultimate. As a truly spiritualized entity, you relate yourself directly with the Ultimate and experience Infinity and being Infinite.

Finite life, with its barriers and limitations, does not cease for the advanced person, but falls into its proper niche as part of the Cosmic Scheme. If you are genuinely aware and spiritually evolved, you do not divorce yourself from life or reject it. By attaining to a high degree of spirituality, you see the Cause-Effect principle behind all of life and are one with the Cosmic Mind Thought Energy from which all stems.

An evolved person transcends life by transmuting it to a greater and higher manifestation. However, you continue operating on the plane of gross matter and by your newly acquired power assist in elevating or raising the vibratory rate of other evolving souls. Since you will know the principle behind all of life, you will unveil its mysteries to those who indicate their readiness and willingness to develop. The knowledge of the Cosmic Laws and Truths becomes the tools with which you can instruct others and through the use of these Laws, demonstrate the practical application of them to your daily living. This also implies your possessing the ability to discern the level of each person, for the Law states, ". . .according to the student's level."

This last principle is very true for anyone who works in the field of occult metaphysics in the dispensing of knowledge. You talk to many groups and individuals as you move upward in spiritual knowledge and evolution, but you must decide what, how, and how much to give to each person or each group. Often, I have had members of the Pompton Lakes Metaphysical Group say, "Now I know why you held back on such and such last year." You must always consider that learning should be a slow, progressive method, for one lesson not fully comprehended or a possible skipping could cause unbalanced awareness or consciousness.

Just this year, a young man who has been with our group for four years passed the remark that he suddenly realized he had gone too far, too fast and had lost his perspective. In his eagerness to *know*, he had missed a little on the way and had not, really, taken sufficient time to digest properly what he had studied. When he saw that confusion had arisen in his thoughts and feelings, he reviewed his position and came to the conclusion that he had to retrace many steps, re-learn, and reapply. His deepest concern centered on what impressions or concepts he might have left with others during the time he had busied himself with tangents rather than the positive Laws and Truths.

Through the centuries, people who involved themselves in the metaphysical approach to life were looked upon as witches, frauds, oddities. The subject of occultism was classified in the realm of the superstitious, and investigation of the supranatural was frowned upon and discouraged. Therefore, mankind not only was limited and trapped in the physical world, but also was prevented from studying what might have been the way to free him from his ignorance and darkness.

Those who concentrated only on the material world did not realize that the world of matter, as a reflection, was not the entire Truth of life and its inhabitants. The mundane world became, in actuality, a prison in which mankind penalized himself—an inescapable trap of his own making.

Now, in the present epoch, you have the opportunities and the knowledge before you in which you can see that this is not true any longer. The material world *is* a reflection, but it goes beyond just a reflection. Probing beneath the exterior manifestation, you discover the reason of being and know that all is a result of the Cause-Effect Principle.

With a renewed metaphysical approach, everything—even the ordinary things in life—assumes meaning and has purpose. The knowledge gleaned by the studying of metaphysics hands you the tools with which to work, to use, to communicate with all the physical aspects of earthly life. The knowledge strips away the bonds of ignorance and frees you from the material limitations.

As a metaphysician and with the knowledge of the Cosmic, the term "supranatural" no longer applies where you are concerned, for you know the explanation behind all that is. Only the not-knowing ascribes the term to what lies behind all of life. This is true, also, of the miracles in all religions, in all countries, and in all periods of time.

Science itself has granted the basis for metaphysical thinking and the destruction of superstitious awe. The scientists' probing into matter altered man's old concepts and placed a mantel of respectability on the theories of what might lie behind all of the manifested world.

When you engage in the spiritual search, you find that you have one fundamental problem. What you once knew and accepted concerning the things in your life and in the physical world of mankind, you now have to change and have to accept new ideas about those things. Old, familiar beliefs must be subjected to reinterpretation. It is a series of new worlds in which you find yourself, and you must adjust to them and cope with the situations and environment of them.

Mystically, you comprehend the old with a newer perspective which shows you the interrelationship of all, the oneness that pervades all life, the Cause and Effect basis for manifestation. All is seen in the term of duality—the Actuality of it and the Reality of it. This means both the tangible and the intangible areas of life. The totality is recognized, not merely some of the segments. Yet, each segment is a totality within itself and is only displaying a certain section.

Possessing the Cosmic Knowledge, you do not see a table *per se*. You are, naturally, aware of the size, shape, design, etc., but in the advanced spiritual state, you know and *see* the atomic structure and the electrons which whirl in space. You relate all of it to all else. The awareness and attention you devote to it focus you on the Reality, but you never ignore the Actuality of what is manifesting on the physical plane.

The complexities of life develop from the attention you place on the wrong or incorrect realities. In acquiring Cosmic Laws and Truths, you can find a balanced Truth. This should be the immediate goal, for much of what you do is characterized by imbalance and runs counter to the basic plan of Nature. Balance is the key-note of the Universe and of Nature; imbalance exists as you and the races of mankind emphasize negativism and increase the accumulated power of all wrong thinking and doing—that of today and of all the yesterdays.

Balance permits you to see the duality of all things and you become aware of the synthesis of life in the Ultimate Plan. Locate your own Balance and it, automatically, pushes aside the limitations and restrictions which are largely due to ignornace.

A good way to attain Balance is to be skeptical about all that enters your mind. Do not reject what appears, but examine it closely; view it objectively from every possible angle, but especially, you should try to review the Cosmic Law that applies. Then, after this scrutiny, you arrive at the truth of what presented itself. You might not particularly appreciate the Truth in it, for the tendency is to reject or ignore that which does not suit. Sincerity of your examination of a thought or idea and dedication to the search for Truth are necessary to follow this method and find Balance.

Balance is seated in the Law of Opposites, which can be refined to Actuality or Reality, Truth or Illusion, Spirit or Matter. Spiritual awareness, in its fullest sense, demands that you observe the two sides of all that exists. Without doing this, you cannot attain the proper perspective.

For example: Does life to you resolve itself only to the material side and not include the spiritual? If so, you are one-sided and in a state of imbalance. On the other hand, as one who attains spirituality, do you concentrate solely on the spiritual and forget the material? This, too, results in a one-sided state of being.

Life cannot be divided with emphasis on one aspect only, for by denying one aspect of life in favor of another, you refute all of life. It cannot exist as a part of itself but in its entirety. Once you realize this, you come to the awareness of duality as being two aspects of ONE. This shows you that every single item of being—animate and inanimate (if there is such)—are but emphasized expressions of one aspect, but contain the potentials of both. Redirection of attention could shift any item from one side to the other—a transmutation or the alchemy of the ancients.

As with the material world and the spiritual world, so it is with you. The sum total of you represents the double phase of the

Cosmic Creation; you are both material, physical and soul, Spirit. Neither should be neglected by too much prominence by the other. Try not to render special consideration to the physical and disregard the spiritual; nor should you stress the spiritual at the expense of the physical. Function in both. Learn the full purpose of Spirit dwelling in matter. Spirit must consider matter important or it would not be, so why should you interpret matter as unimportant?

Your aim should be to coalesce the physical and the spiritual, the outer and the inner, and create the Balance which brings you the solution to living, the peace, the development you seek. The amount of success, of course, depends upon the often repeated guides of sincere desire and true effort on your part.

It is almost as if you have to double-think to observe this duality. Naturally, it is not easy, for you have been accustomed to placing your mind on one or the other—according to your social and cultural heritage and experiences in life. It does not mean a shifting back and forth such as a pendulum, but a standing in the middle, seeing both sides of everything at the same time.

Often you might wonder why humanity struggles so and engages in all the strife of living when the solutions to life are readily available and so plentiful. The reason for it all rests in the evolutionary pattern established according to the principles of the Cosmos. You, usually, are not too aware or conscious of the Truth, and so flounder through life's experiences. Purpose exists in this, for growth implies certain painful times. Through the experience of *unknowingness* of Truth can be derived a state of what has been termed "conscious awareness of Truth."

You hardly know yourself so how can you know Truth? By becoming "self"-aware, you become aware of Truth, for within your Real Self is the Real Truth.

You are fortunate that you are part of the New Age Cycle, for it brings to all an opportunity to expand consciousness to a universality with all. In this New Age, the soul consciousness within you will embrace far greater power than the atomic bomb and has the potential of annihilating warfare. With the experience will be the awareness of greater Truth and the greater expansion of Truth. As you become conscious of this spiritual source, you are a part of and not apart from everything and everyone. No longer should you ever feel alone, for you are in everything and everything is in you.

This expansion of all consciousness refers to the Universes as well. The discovery by astronomers of what they labelled "Blue Quaziers" seems to indicate that the galaxies are in the same program of growth. This is what Alice Bailey hinted at in her autobiography when she stated that the entire universe is in a constant state of ever-expanding and that the Over-Soul is in the identical condition. One author once remarked that the universe expands outwardly and finally returns to itself—a sort of heavenly prodigal son. It reminds you, too, of the Cosmic Law—"As above, so below." Too, you recall the outbreathing and the inbreathing, the act of Creativity, and the withdrawing of its powers. Could the pauses be likened to the seventh day of rest?

Find your way in life. That is what seems to be lacking in most lives—the goals, the direction. There are many guides to follow in finding this way. Science is beginning to help. Remember that Einstein's theory of relativity resulted in the splitting of the atom. When you discover a law, as the men of science do, use it where it is applicable, but do not confine it solely there. You might see that it also can be used elsewhere. Principles and Laws apply specifically, but in addition, are universal, eternal, and all-encompassing in all areas of the manifested and unmanifested lives.

Through these guides, principles, Laws, etc., you can find the means whereby you can strike upon a pathway, but it will be an individual discovery. No one can do it for you. It might seem a singular path, separate from all others, but as you evolve and move ahead, you will see that every spoke on the wheel leads to the hub or the center of all life.

One great step to take is to participate actively in life. By the act of involvement, you live and breathe in unison with the forces that are the real source behind life. Participation means, here, the application of the Cosmic Laws and Truths to daily life for your own particular evolvement and for the betterment of your fellow man.

Most of you are "dead" in life. How active are you really? On what phases of living are your efforts concerned? You think in terms of securities, families, social life, pleasures, but are these areas sufficient as outlets for creative activity? To some of you it is being creative, and in some ways they can serve depending upon the chances to employ the Laws and Truths in these sections or departments of life. Usually, the general run-of-the-mill life centers on just those things as ordinary, daily living, but not involving creativity.

The majority of you are learners in the world, leaning upon your material possessions such as homes, money, job position, social standing, etc. Are these the things upon which your values are placed? Where would you be if they suddenly were removed from you? Regarding your religious beliefs, would they assist you in times of stress and turmoil and death? Basically, can you cope with the everyday problems that exist within your special environment?

Throughout all of these situations and questions, the chief concern is whether or not you remain, spiritually, at-one-ment with the Ultimate despite all that occurs around you. The Balance that you attain to in soul evolvement would or should be the main spring in your efforts to be rhythmically synchronized and in harmony with the Universes. It all refers back to the Law of Balance, the recognition of the principle of duality.

Individually you have to arrive at this state: knowing the powers that are behind all the manifested world, being at-one-ment with these powers, remaining a co-worker of the Absolute in the material world. This Balance of materiality and spirituality is a goal for which each of you should earnestly strive to reach so that your lives will then reflect the harmony of a balanced existence.

Concentrate on the awareness of your spiritual heritage and potentials and the role of being human in a physical, tangible world. No road in the life will be a fearsome journey when you reach this level of understanding, for you then substitute wisdom for fears, harmony, for strife, balance for chaos. Your auric field displays then an appearance of wholeness or completeness in Cosmic Truth, Law, and Order.

Chardin illustrated very clearly in his HYMN OF THE UNIVERSE that there is the Oneness that is contained in all things, that the Absolute is involved in everything and is everywhere. Wherever you look, you know that the Ultimate is present. As the Ultimate, then, is everywhere and in everything, it should be the incentive for you to solve the problems of your material existence.

The only thing you have to do is to know yourself. Realize that you are a Finite Being in so far as the lower part of the duality is concerned. By the lower is not implied a negative, minor quality, but is meant the opposite duality. However, you are also an Infinite Being with all the attributes and qualities of the Absolute. Many people might consider the Finite Being as the lesser of the duality and the Infinite Being as the greater. This is true, in a sense, but not that the Finite Being is unimportant. It is extremely important for it is the channel of expression for the degree to which the Infinite Being expresses itself in the evolutionary process.

Education is an evolutionary process also. The fifth grade, for example, is *higher* than the fourth, but could you function on the fifth grade level if you had not gone through the learning steps of the fourth? It is an unusual person who can. Thus, the Finite Being and the Infinite Being are equal in that each fulfills a segment of the Universal Plan of the Cosmos. By spiritual alchemy, the Finite Being becomes the Infinite Being.

As you have evolved through the ages to this point, you have always been aware of the restlessness within you—the endless search for Reality, for the reason of being. Although you have been trapped in the physical world by attention to the sense perceptive world, there has ever been an unknown factor of something more, that life is more than just the physical. The progressive experiences of each incarnation impressed you, little by little, of this until you are now at the stage of not only being aware of the Infinite qualities of life and of yourself, but also that you can reach the state in which you are with the Infinite and can identify yourself with it.

Of course, you waver, even here, for doubts assail you. You need proof of it to possess a feeling of security in it all. Throughout the annals of history, how many have really known themselves? Highlighting the historical archives are men such as Jesus, Confuscius, Buddha, who could resist the desires of the sense-perceptive faculties and know themselves in the Reality of their Being. All of them proved their oneness with the Absolute. Jesus, said, "I and the Father are One."

All of these leaders exemplified the Cosmic on earth—an expression of the Cosmic Energy in the flesh—"The Word made flesh." And in each one, death was conquered in their immortality by demonstrating the power of Spirit over matter. Each was the epitome of the duality.

The drive that was in each of those Masters should be in you, the drive to express the Infinite within. You possess the identical spiritual faculties that they had, but you have yet to learn the application of these faculties so that you can express Truth to the same degree. You are, in Reality, Spirit and Matter, God and Man. Both are equal in quality, and the characteristics of one are in the other. Find your own path to the eventual and inevitable manifestation of the Balance of the double aspect.

Can prayer be of assistance to you? Very possibly, but this will depend upon how much you know what prayer is and how to use it correctly. Prayer in religion today has deteriorated into a pleading for help, for things. You beseech the Ultimate for the solution to your problems, forgetting that the Absolute is impartial, for if He gives to one, He must give to all. Actually, why ask God for anything? The Cosmic Supply is available and unlimited when you know how to obtain it.

When you ask God for something, you place a barrier between God and you, for the act of requesting indicates that you are unaware of the powers that you have and the Oneness with the Creator. It is the ignorance and the darkness surrounding you which limits and causes to appear a gulf between the Creator and His creation. The Cosmic knows what transpires in all lives, in all things, yet remains impersonal.

Prayer should have as its goal the unification of the parts of the whole. What it really is is a method of concentration and meditation in which you raise your consciousness to meet that of the Absolute. Spirit in matter must increase its awareness to equal that of pure Spirit. The act of praying is thus an individual matter and needs no outside influence, such as a church, a statue, etc. These are ritualistic features which cause confusion to some and malign the very purpose of prayer. Too often, you confuse the external features as the Truth instead of the symbol of the Truth.

My grandfather was an exceptionally fine man in character and values and standards. People came from all over to sit and to talk with him, for he was a very learned man (yet had only two years of formal education). He once remarked that he never went to church, for to him, the Lord was everywhere. When he needed to establish contact with the Deity, he could do so in his home, his garden, his work shop. He also stated that he never asked God for anything—just assistance in guiding him on the right way. Grandfather felt that the Lord was subject to too many petitions of "give me this; give me that." Life was my grandfather's responsibility, not the Deity's.

Another interesting statement he once made was that the Lord does not judge you by what you do but by what you are. This is a provocative remark because it implies judgment being doled out according to the level upon which each person is. Of course, his observation in this could be much disputed and also used as an alibi by many. However, close examination of it should evidence the Truth within it. You cannot equate the behavior patterns of the savage with the behavior of the so-called civilized man. An unevolved soul has yet to learn. The evolved soul should have learned and is judged by the progress and the application of the Cosmic Principles to life. The *knowing* is the vital factor. Not knowing is excusable *beyond* the level of the development. At the level of development (since all is graded experience and knowledge) each is judged.

Let us return again to prayer. To many, prayer is the contact with God, the Father. But, is it contact or worship? The question arises as to whether or not you should worship God, for it makes you a quality lesser than that from which you had your source. Recognition of the Infinite might be a better word, but with the recognition should be an accompanying realization that you are a part of God in the making.

Do you need external features to assist you in contacting the Supreme? This could be decided upon the basis of your own development or awareness. Some people need the ritualistic ceremonies to guide them; others resent ritual. Within itself, for those who are beginners, rituals could help, but the tendency might arise to attend the *acts* of the ritual rather than the meaning behind them. Rituals seem to confine themselves, after periods of time, into tradition and law and thus result in limitations.

Contact with the Higher Self, the Supreme, should be from the consciousness of sincere search for Truth. This will cause no separation or barriers, but brings you to attunement with the Creative Element. Just the ordinary experience of daily life gives you the opportunity to communicate with the Absolute, for all experiences are effective when you identify them with Oneness and with *Be-ness*.

There is no one place in which to establish contact with the Higher Self — the still, small voice within. Listening to great music offers many chances, for your attention to the beautiful strains raises your vibrations to a higher level. Nature abounds with media of contact — a beautiful sunset, a single petal of a flower, even the thunder clouds become a thing of admiration despite the fact that they herald an approaching storm.

Go within yourself to establish rapport with the Ultimate. There might be some delay or detours, for the ego might interfere. Lack of knowledge and poor judgment could prevent achievement too. You have to de-personalize yourself, become quiet, and meditate.

When you do this, you are involved with meditation techniques, which in themselves, are fine, but do not get greatly involved with ritualistic or physical methods of preparation. No method or technique is really that important. As you are ready in your meditation, the Truth should appear to you. The Truth could be encouraged by you if you contemplate on a great thought or a Cosmic Principle. This will raise your vibrations, for you have your attention on the right and the correct. Remember that you must also maintain a continuity of effort which is important. Do not vacillate or you will never achieve this communication or attunement with Higher Truth.

All this is possible for you, but the success of it will depend upon how much you have learned of Truth and how much you apply the Cosmic Laws to life. Do you dwell too much in the past or live too much for the future? The ever-present "now" is the important thing to concern yourself with. It is the prosaic events of life that will provide the means to construct your character and your development. If you look to that which has happened or seek only what will happen, you could miss what *is* happening.

The Reality of "now", the present, should be where you are—mentally, spiritually, physically. When you get out of harmony with the "now", then the imbalance upsets your poise of the present. Your life becomes chaotic; disagreeable events occur, for you are out-of-step with the present, and the job-at-hand, the "now", is the most important where time is considered.

None of this implies that you completely ignore the past nor stop planning the future. You need to recognize the past to understand the present and in understanding the present and working with it, you automatically *know* what the future will be.

Take each day and each moment of living and live it wholly and fully. Each day is new and different and so is each moment. The day and the moment involve the entire pattern of Laws and Truths. You should live each day in as much awareness as is possible, where you are with what you have developed.

The present is not merely a stepping stone—it is the "now" the right time for Truth. Truth is not only found nor is it limited to just the past, present, or future; otherwise, it would not be Infinite. Spiritual Infinity is that which was, is, and will be as an eternal self-fulfillment. Every moment is endowed with eternal significance, and it is not the theory of Truth but the practice of it which counts in the spiritual life.

Learn how to use your emotions whether negative or positive, but do not permit the negative emotions to merely work themselves off and neither should you repress or suppress them. Giving in to emotions and mental disturbances brings about an imbalanced state with varied degrees of confusion and if you continually live within the center of your emotions and make no effort to monitor them, the emotions will rule you.

Remember that each soul dwells in a different human form and makes its own heaven or hell, here and now. Each is a complete law within itself, punished and rewarded as it winds its way through the evolutionary process hourly and daily. It learns through its own experiences here on earth. Your soul has always lived and has always had a conscious being, and your soul gives new powers in direct proportion to its expansive capacity. It is an eternal aspect of Spirit within you and goes on eternally. In rare instances, the Soul can *think* itself out of existence by ceasing or refusing to recognize itself and its potentials or its Oneness with the Source. When this happens, it rejoins the Sea of Cosmic Root Substance from which it came in the beginning.

Each of you understands things, events, and circumstances in proportion to the degree of your awakened consciousness. This achievement of awareness or consciousness is commensurate with the effort you supply. By what you do now, you condition your future in this life, and make your place in the next world. All planes exist here *now*. If you would but realize this, you might be more zealous in putting your world in order. Think about right action in your life, for every action is intimately related to your progress.

The substance with which you work is very plastic and easily conforms to that form which you desire. You may build a palace as easily as a sand pile formed by a child into different shapes. Your thought power is the instrument that shapes and blends colors in all forms you create. So, when all is right, then the good you accomplish has been rewarded; when all is confusion, the negative accomplishment is punished. All follow the Law of Compensation.

There is a Cosmic Energy free to all from which you receive power to use which will result in better relationships with all. It rests within the Cosmic Law of Harmony, the "Love of God." The force is vital and potent, free-flowing, and magnetically attractive to you when you are ready to use it correctly. To use this Cosmic Energy would mean that you have eliminated the negative thoughts and emotions from your consciousness. But how do you arrive to this state?

Think of the emotion of anger. It is fairly easy to control the outward expression of anger but difficult to manage the inward turmoil of the feeling created. Every one of your nerves is "set on edge" and time is required before this situation subsides and your mind returns to customary equanimity. If you wish to regulate anger, attack it at the beginning before it has time to gain momentum. Anger spreads with amazing rapidity throughout the brain and the nervous system. It summons to its side all the emotions and instincts akin to it. So, the control of it is most important. Turn the mind aside from the angry mood.

Everytime your emotions are stirred, more particularly when stirred unpleasantly, study how you can profit by the experience. Start being critical and analytical with yourself—making yourself the object of study. In this way, you often might forget the cause of your anger which cannot exist at the same time with your practice of reasoning, nor can you think calmly when angry. Giving way to unrestrained anger is very dangerous, for it exhausts you physically and subjects your nervous systems to many disorders. If you are prone to becoming angry, you should learn the value of a calm, cool, collected attitude of mind. Try fixing your attention on your breathing. When you are angry, your breath is short and quick. Practice deep breathing until the emotions are controlled.

Do not blame negative conditions on someone else. All circumstances start from yourself and by the Law of Attraction, bring similar environmental factors to you. If you think in terms of revenge, retaliation, destruction, you are out-of-harmony with the Cosmos. There are no negativisms in the Cosmic, but the negative elements arise from the self-created world of yourself — not the Cosmic. You have but to keep yourself at-one with the Higher Forces, and all will be right and evolve correctly. Even the nations of the world reflect the forces which emanate from the people.

As you comprehend that all Truth is in the Cosmic and in you, you experience new expansions of consciousness. You are God individualized and are Truth, which is the realization of the Absolute within the individualized manifestation. You are that spark of the Deity, but in self-imposed conditions.

Now, the *effects* of causes themselves becomes *causes*, for in the cycle of manifestation, there is nothing static or fixed or finally determined. Do not be mislead by apparent moments of achievement; they are but prefaces to change, for such is the Law of Being.

There is an unseen hand or inner guidance for all of you. It is a prompting from the Great Presence within you and is always accessible to you as you follow the right path and try to live constructively. Daily analyze your thoughts; correct your faults, wrong attitudes, and work habits. As you understanding of the Cosmic Laws unfolds, you become aware of the discriminating intelligence becoming more powerful.

When you live in the Reality of *now*, this minute, this hour, you are living in Truth. There is a time for everything — a time to be born, to die, to work, to play. It is the organization or the *order* that you bring to your daily activities that makes your life easier. Although nothing is the same as it was a minute ago, each thing, in its own time and place, has the element of Truth within.

The forms which contain the life-energies do not change, just the conditions surrounding these forms, so that the life-forces within can express what is necessary for growth. The forms *are* the result of consciousness and Mind which express through the forms that they attract through the inherent quality of the consciousness and the Mind. So, what form you are inhabiting today is the harvest of your consciousness and thoughts of all your yesterdays. Tomorrow's shapes will be the testimony of what you thought, felt, and did today.

As you live for Truth and sincerely apply Cosmic Laws to living, you refine the essence of the present form and prepare the one you will be using in the future lives. Your "now" is the conditioning factor for your tomorrows.

The emphasis on "nowness" cannot be underrated, for it is basic to every possible progress. What you are *now* and what you, at this time, do *now* is you in the future tense. Existence, at all times, rests on the "now".

Matter is Spirit formed. You have to conceive the concept that *being* is a cause. Everything that exists has some source of *be-ness* with qualities and characteristics which find forms through which to express. The form will be equal to the level of your highest consciousness and your Mind. The Reality of Being sits in the Supreme, which appears as all that is.

Common mistakes that you make result from the fact that you see all things in their *actuality*, the external appearances in other words. As mentioned previously, the outer is the temporary and subject to the immutable Law of Change. "Things are not what they seem" as the old saying goes. The "things" and their corresponding forms, which are readily observed, serve only as the means for the inner to express its inherent potentialities. In your ignorance, you place great importance on the outer (actuality) and ignore the inner (reality).

Only when you go within a person, a thing, a circumstance will you come to the knowledge of the Reality of it. For the inner is the only real and eternal part of you that lives through all of your lifetimes.

Placing attention on what has been said or what has been done by someone is focusing on the outer aspect. You see the effect or the condition and that is what you are really dealing with. You will, of course, blame the person—that is, if you have *not* evolved yourself where you can look within. However, as an evolved soul, you could see the cause which underlies the effect.

When you evaluate a person or a thing—not in the sense of judging but in analyzing—you should look to the inner person and not the outer. The outer does not give you the Reality of Truth about the person or the thing. Also, as you evaluate the person, let us say, what are you viewing? Remember that he is only expressing something, but is that the real person? Perhaps as you analyze it, the condition of the person is what you see and are not seeing the real *him*.

Too, do you permit any of the things that a person does or the circumstances in life disturb you? What a person says or does really is not the real "he" many times The Law of Discrimination teaches you to view the acts or words with compassion and complete understanding.

It is not meant, however, that you allow people to say and to do anything to you to the extent of harm. You must not be that humble or detache that people take advantage of you. Know why the person acts the way he does according to the level of his development, but do not, for his sake as well as for yours, demean yourself or be taken advantage of. There is a time to say "no" and a time to let the other person know that he has gone far enough and that he can go no further. This can be accomplished without any difficulty or any unpleasantness. Yours is the responsibility to see to it that it is done properly, for you know better and you know the way. The greatest lessons are taught through firmness, tact, diplomacy.

Most people are enmeshed in a web of ignorance. Their actions, thoughts and feelings reflect this state. In your case, if evolved, the detachment from their circumstances and the effects of their living will prevent you from being influenced. The 91st Psalm is so often used as an aid or a guide, and certainly applies in this particular circumstance—it will not "come nigh thee"—according to the emplacement of your consciousness and where you have placed your attention.

It cannot be emphasized too many times or too strongly that you are Body, Mind, and Spirit—the Trinity of Self, yet all is One with the Ultimate. This is well represented in the lower triangle of the six-pointed Star of David or the Seal of Solomon. The Oneness of the triplicity should be the focal point from which you energize all the thoughts and feelings and actions which are expressed in the manifested Universe.

There are other interpretations to the points of the lower triangle. One author stated that one point represented the Son (Christ, the love principle). The second is the Truth of God, and the third is life itself with all of the experiences contained therein.

All of this might be confusing, for you must envision the triangles as being the Body, Mind, Spirit (Triplicity of Self) and God, the Son, and Life (Triplicity of Cosmic Energy). Most of you will need much time to become One with the Infinite, and you see all aspects of the Finite world. The duality of creation evidences itself in these two triangles. The adepts who have had their Initiation see the whole of all.

The Be-ness and Is-ness of all life have their source in the Supreme—the Universal Mind—God. The term associated with the Infinite is not important—only the recognition of the existence of the Cosmos. All of life revolves around and exists within this

Supreme Being. The physical life is the manifestation of the Great Force and, actually, is not limited. The limitations and the transitory appearances of life exist only because of the incorrect and misapplication of Cosmic Laws and Truth.

It is all there — just look for it. Seek the immortal, eternal Spirit that dwells within you — the "I am presence", containing all that was, is, or ever shall be. This Eternal Spirit is the beginning (alpha) and the ending (omega) of all life and all intelligence.

Awareness of this spiritual force within you will lead you to the greatest experience you could ever know. When this occurs, your life will improve for you, personally, and for all of those in your environment. There will be continuous growth and development — no more delays, postponements, or obstacles to overcome.

The duality of existence will unite within the One, for Reality will be the dominant feature in your life. Self-mastery must be attained through experiencing all facets of living, all experiences. Ignore nothing; apply all knowledge and Truth.

The whole of life will become more meaningful as you live from the center within. Remember that you are Gods in the Making.

MYSTICAL EXPERIENCES

What is a mystical experience for one may seem to be a coincidence, illusion, phenomena or fantasy for others. Writers on the subject, even those who may have personal knowledge of such experience, readily admit the inadequacy of their descriptions.

Words flatten the mystical experience, and the fact is understandable when you track the origin of the word "mystic." Its Greek root "mustes" suggests that the mystical experience must remain secret and incommunicable. Its contributory root "muo" translates simply: "I shut my mouth (and close my eyes)."

Mystical experiences are felt and known, not described and related. After all of the rationalization, examination and intellection of the experience is over, the experience remains only knowable to the experiencer—still not explainable, still not describable, probably not repeatable; just knowable.

This suggests that an experiencer of a real mystical experience would be less frustrated by his inability to communicate it than the experiencer of illusion or phenomena. The mystic knows; he knows that he knows, and that's enough.

Before you can attain to any mystical experience, you must arrive at a point of view that ascertains the conviction that the power behind all of the manifested world is the Absolute Mind. This is very necessary for certain steps to take and certain questions to resolve which will form the basis of dedicated belief.

The Absolute is not beyond your reach. You need not contemplate on the heavens and envision the Ultimate as being "beyond" here and located "out there." The Ultimate is ever-present and is the all-pervading essence or energy behind all.

In order to experience a mystical state, it becomes necessary to recognize the transcendental reality of the Absolute and to attempt (successfully, of course) to establish a personal contact with this Reality. Once having accomplished the contact, you then relate the experience to the mundane affairs of your life.

You might question the reason behind the relating of the experience to everyday life. Many feel that the contact with the Absolute is an individual experience for them only and for their specific spiritual evolvement. This is very true, but remember that all is for the good of all, and the higher you evolve, the more you can contribute to the development of the entire human race as well as the members of the lower forms of being. The contact with the Absolute is meant to be an individual happening, but it is not a selfish one or should not be selfish.

Oneness implies the sharing of knowledge and experiences, but not in the shape of example only. Any contact with Higher Forces or the Cosmos is something you cannot describe to another, but the effect on you and the reflection in your attitudes and in your ways of living, from then on, serve as a goal for others.

It is not easy to translate the understanding that you arrive at, in a practical way, to those who have yet to encounter or to arrive at this level of development. You can only hint at what will occur in everyone's life if each strives for the spiritual advancement and comes to this Initiation (contact with God).

Occult metaphysics strongly affirms that the possibility of establishing a definite contact with the Supreme Being is a Reality which anyone may attain if he strives strongly in the disciplines of the Cosmic Laws and Truths. The Absolute is not beyond the reach of any spiritualized unit of Its own consciousness. Since each of you is a segment of the Universal Mind, there is no separation from it where you are concerned. Apparent separation exists because you are out-of-harmony with the Cosmic Principles and have erected a barrier which prevents communication. You are the only person who can re-establish this communication, for the channel to the Absolute is always open and clear. Your end of the contact is clogged and muddled by the negative forces of thought, feeling, and action that you permit to be the dominant and ruling characteristics of your life.

Consummate the Reality of the contact with the Absolute. Your sole aim in life should always be directed to this goal. It *is* the main purpose of the soul's many journeys, through its incarnations, on the physical plane. You should be constantly attempting to extend yourself to the realization of the contact.

Naturally, you will wish to know how you can establish this contact or connection with the Absolute, and if there are some guidelines which you could follow. Primarily, you realize, that the connection with the Absolute is a personal one and an individual one for you and for you only. Therefore, since you are, in essence, a mental being, reason should be the first prerequisite as a means to approach what is not just a contact but is really a re-unification with the Ultimate. Reasoning is an innate faculty which all of you possess, and it is also part of the Universal or World Mind.

As you consciously develop your innate reasoning qualities, you are able to see the entire Cosmic Pattern and clearly understand the evolutionary process and purpose in the Cosmic. This reasoning state is not easily come by, but through the experiences in life, through your studying, and through your application of Cosmic Laws and Truths, you will eventually be able to observe the intelligence in the scope and plan of manifested being.

The intelligence you use stems directly from the Cosmic Mind, and its proper use is indicative of initial unfoldment in you. With this intelligence, coupled with Cosmic Knowledge, you begin to be a conscius spiritualized unit which assists in the evolutionary design of the Cosmos. This also implies you ability to understand the various levels of development of all members of the race and enables you to work with them according to their respective stations on the evolutionary ladder. You recognize the fact that all are on different levels of development and you accept each one where he is.

The Cosmic Law of Acceptance is most important in mystical experience. You learn to accept each experience that comes to you and see it in its perspective of occult metaphysical teachings. From these, you see the relationship of experience to your spiritual growth. You know your place in the physical world which then, in turn, becomes accepted, for now you know the why and wherefor of more being where you are. Every single mystical experience should clarify more and more the mysteries of life and your reason for being.

The intellectual basis of your existence provides the means to free yourself from the prejudices and ego-centered areas. Through this, you guide yourself into adequate conduct, proper understanding, a developed and active intuition. Intuitive faculties reside in every one of you, but in most of you it is very latent. This force is a transcendental quality when developed and used properly. The correct use of the intellect enables you to see everything, and with this comes the solving of the whole problem of the Universe, its Cause and Effect, its purpose.

It has been stated before that as you come to the realization of one Truth, you find still more Truths beyond and beyond those Truths are even more. With your increased development of your spirituality, you advance from Truth to Truth. However, the question arises as whether you are discovering new Truths or arriving at an expanded consciousness of the Truth itself. Too, you might ask if these intellectual concepts that you arrive at are the Real Truth. Intellectual concepts are not the same as the Real Truth, for they can be colored by your interpretations.

Your concepts of Truth vary according to values, your learning, and your experiences. Since all of learning is a series of progressive steps, based mainly upon life's experiences, your concepts of Truth will shift accordingly. This is why Truth *is* flexible to the degree that segments of it can be applied to each stage of your evolvement, and yet, as only a segment, will not detract from the Ultimate Truth when you arrive at the point where you see it in its totality.

Also, intellectual concepts are conditioned by the racial and cultural heritage to which you are subjected. Once you fully evolve out of the limiting factors involved in race and culture, you reach beyond to the higher, fuller Truth. The shadings of degrees of Truth do not distract from the qualities of Truth but exemplify the justice of the application of the Cosmic Laws and Truths to the evolutionary pattern of being.

As you move into higher and higher Truths, you will develop a relationship with Truth. This is greater than your identification of Truth, for by placing yourself in a relationship with it, you become part of it and its functioning. In an identification status, you emphasize the duality—Truth and You; whereas with a relationship with Truth, you and the Truth are One.

Too often, those of you who seek a mystical experience in this study confuse the personality with the inner "I Am" or the Higher Self. You seem, almost, unaware of your Higher Self and perpetuate ideals and concepts based upon personality awareness. Remember that the personality is only the projected aspect of the Real You in the physical plane (the involuted Higher Self). It represents the opposite polarity (lower self), and you must take all precautionary measures to assure that it does not assume the greater role of the two aspects. Your Higher Self can operate through the personality if you consciously tune the outer to reflect the inner.

If you emphasize the outer at the expense of the inner, the Higher Self retreats and waits for further development of a spiritual awakening. The energy of the Higher Self continues its consistent flow and might be considered the "voice of conscience," for it ever strives to impress you of its existence and the potentialities within it.

The outer self (personality) dwells in the world of materiality, the sense-perceptive world, the illusory existence. So long as the person focuses attention on the value of the mundane areas to the neglect of the spiritual, you will be plunged into the worrisome and fearful problems of daily living. They are worrisome and fearful because by the act of placing too much value and attention upon them, you magnify the physical experiences beyond their proper perspective.

All of your physical living experiences should be to grant you the opportunities to learn and evolve, but by wrong attention, you often miss the essential point or the essence of the lesson. Because you look only to the outward side of life and not to the inward side, the temporary glamor, the transient qualities of life claim you and are responsible for the lack of growth. Life is an ever-changing spectacle upon which you can hardly ever gain a firm grasp or a firm sense of security.

When Spirit descended into matter, it was early and easily provided with the necessary forms of each kingdom through which to express itself adequately according to level and specie. These forms were equipped with the essential tools to work on the physical plane. The five sense provided, and still provide, mankind with the machinery to experience the world of matter in all of its characteristics. These five senses are most necessary to those of you who are experiencing tangible life, but do not exclude the opposite polarity—Spirit. Spirit, within you, has the Higher Self as its tool to work with and through on this level of existence.

You hinder the Higher Self from performing as a channel for Spirit when you concentrate solely on the bodily senses. You extrovert your attention from the duality aspect of your Reality and practically deny the Inner You its recognition, awareness, and operation. By so doing, the Higher Self becomes a prisoner of the outer shell and cannot possibly perceive of life and its experiences, for you have shut it out and it cannot grow as it should.

How could the Higher Self manage to remain the most forceful energy within you and demonstrate itself and its latent power? It must have the dominion over all of you and all of your life and its activities. The five sense must become sublimated or subservient to it or, at least, transmuted into transcendental qualities in the physically manifested world. The Higher Self within you then supplies the knowledge, the understanding, the guidelines for you to become a co-worker with the Creator—"You do your Father's work." You live from the heart center through the Law of Harmony, and by increasing your vibratory rate, you are an example of Spirit, and you affect all within your sphere of influence.

Paying attention to the external world features grants you many opportunities to learn and to grow through these experiences encountered in your everyday living. However, the absorption of the lessons involved could be delayed if the Higher Self is ignored. Attention should be both extroverted (to the visible, tangible world) and introverted (to the invisible worlds), and thus, you step further along a pathway to Balance. Too often, a higher percentage of attention to the physical world can confuse you in seeking the Reality of Life, which is located within the Higher Self.

Awareness must be of an inner perspective, not an outer one, for it actually resolves itself to introspection of a positive and constructive nature. To have Balance, however, the outer and the inner must coalesce so that each knows the other in its proper niche and purpose of Being. To some of you, this might seem rather peculiar and bordering on the ridiculous, but when you review the principle of duality, you will see that no Balance is possible or probable without the co-existence of both aspects of you, plus the recognition of both segments of each other.

The materialist sees only the one aspect and considers it as the Reality since it falls into the category of the sense-perceptive faculties. If you are one who advocates materiality as the basis of life, you prevent yourself from conceiving of the fundamentals which underlie the manifestation of the physical appearances in life. Life, then, to the materialist centers only in that which can be detected through the five senses. Beyond that, to him, there is nothing.

Transcendental mysticism refutes the position of the physical attentions. To the true mystic, the physically minded or sense oriented person "cannot see the forest for the trees," As a transcendentalist, you will know and experience the introspection that is most necessary for complete spiritual awareness. You can not only reach the proofs of the ancients, but also experiment yourself with the techniques and methods that will bring you to the state of awareness which gives you the transcendental introspection.

Naturally, as a novice in the field of true mystical experience, you must establish the proper conditions which will provide the right channels for mysticism. Self-awareness unfolds as you gradually become alert to the power within you and learn how to use it in Truth. Merely exhibiting an interest in this subject is not sufficient grounds to declare yourself a mystic. You arrive at the status of a true mystic when you have learned enough, applied enough, experienced enough to know and appreciate the value of a transcendental occurrence in your life. If and when this happens to you, you will know and your life will be a reflection of the practical philosophy and attitudes and knowledge of the mystics.

Of course, you must realize that you have to prepare yourself in some ways to achieve the mystical experience and to become a real and a true mystic. Philosophically, you can delve into the mental machinations of theory, possibility, etc., and this should actually be the primary step. You must be mentally aware of the potentials, mentally willing to accept and experience the events which will transpire in your life, mentally recognize the existence of that "something other" which man has sought through all eternity.

Realize, first, that the usual methods that you have employed in the attainment of knowledge and skills might not be applicable in this special study, for you are no longer dealing with the common, ordinary aspects of physical living. The Mind itself might often have to be pushed aside to allow the higher centers to function and bring comprehension of the mystical approach to life. Intrinsically, the very nature of what you seek automatically excludes dependence upon the five physical senses to grasp and to know.

How can you come to the realization of what it is that you seek and what you might need to use in order to reach and understand it? Basically, it is your Intuition (a much misunderstood and misused word) that will be the main avenue of approach to this long-sought goal. Many people employ the term "insight," but this merely brings on a debate about semantics. Intuition and insight could easily be considered one and the same, for in using it in a developed form, you are able to see all life as it really is — all things, all beings. You do not rivet attention on the outer appearances — the illusion or the glamor — but gear all faculties to observing and to becoming aware of the Reality, the permanent, the eternal qualities.

What you see when you only observe the external is the physical manifestation of the Reality. The physical qualities have been imposed upon you by virtue of the necessity of functioning on the physical plane. Evolvement spiritually enables you to "go behind the scenes" and investigate the inner Reality. Once you know this, you can align yourself with the life essence of all life on all planes in all galaxies.

Your Higher Self must be placed in a position where it will hold dominion over all areas of your being. Within the Higher Self is the

home of the Intuition, the Insight. As the physical body has its channels through which to observe and experience life, so does the
Spiritual Body have its own. Sight in the physical realm enables you
to see and through seeing, to analyze, to evaluate what comes to
your view. Naturally, you know the limitations of physical sight in
so far as distance and detail are concerned. In so far as the Mind is
concerned, the intellect, in its own way, sees, observes, evaluates.
Thus, it becomes the channel for the Mental Body. The Intuition or
Insight belongs to the higher Self and represents the channel
through which the Higher Self functions in seeing, observing,
evaluating. Thus it is that all the bodies on all the levels contain the
essential equipment which permits these bodies in the problem of
adjusting to the specific level with the Laws of Being for each level.

Intuition, really, is the entrance or doorway to the knowledge
of a transcendental character. When you come to the use of this
faculty, you have arrived at a stage of development in which you
now will know all the answers to the principle of creation and the
problems of life, for the purpose and the Cosmic Plan is unfolded
before you through your intuition and insight. It is here, too, that
the experiences of the physical world and the experiences of the
spiritual world are united as One. It is the unity of the whole with
the sum total of all of its parts coalesced in an advanced state of
consciousness. What was never known or felt is placed before you
so that you can see the completeness of all things in the manifested
world.

Your Mind is a conscious force within you, and you must come
to the realization that it is through this force that you will eventually experience a transcendental event within the intellect. Any
transcendental experience must fall into this stage, for without the
Mind to accept and analyze it, the experience would be of no value.
The transcendental experience should be of a positive nature when
coupled with Mind realization. It is also worth mentioning at this
point that all mystical experiences should incorporate a degree of
the Mind or much could be missed without the scrutiny of Mind being involved.

Realization through the Mind faculty will result in "Reality
Realization" or awareness. The awareness makes the mystical experience a very personal one, vivid and potent and indicates to you
the practicality of it in your every day life. All mystical experience
must relate to your life in the physical world and from there extend
itself to your spiritual world or all of your invisible worlds and
bodies.

Intellectual concepts and the awareness of these concepts are fine within themselves but hardly sufficient when it comes to mystical experience itself. No knowledge, no transcendental occurrence can be meaningful unless applicable to life, for of what value is any of this if it is not used in the problem of living? The purpose of all of life is the application of the Cosmic Laws and Truths to the problems you have and to the development of your spiritual faculties. None of it can be done unless all that you learn is practically applied in everyday events. Growth and progress are marked only as you successfully put all knowledge and mystical experience into use as you live day by day.

Too many who seek the Empyrean Heights reject their earthly existence — perhaps hoping that by so ignoring it, it might go away. Mystical experience does not, and never will, advocate your withdrawal from the affairs of the mundane world but rather emphasizes the necessity of propelling yourself more deeply into earthly existence. Mystical experiences will come more easily when you gain the proper perspective and conquer life in a constructive and correct manner.

Many discussions rage in metaphysical groups as to what method is better in order to attain to an enlightenment which will produce mystical experiences. There are those who advocate working within — the interior you, the Higher Self, and from there, the outer will be affected and will manifest the Inner You. Another group seems to feel that you must first work on the outer and then reach into the Inner Self, making it a sort of purification process before approaching the altar, so to speak.

Does it really matter which is followed so long as the stage for mystical experience is arrived at? You can present many agruments pro and con for either method, but, in reality, on what is your attention — the method or the goal? In my estimation, either is of value so long as it suits the spiritual growth of the individual. Each finds the way according to his specific level of development and selects the method most comfortable and most rewarding to him. Personally, I advance the approach from the Outer to the Inner. It reminds me of the theory involved in the homeopathic medical approach to illnesses. The illnesses, according to homeopathic doctors and diagnosticians who are also interested in metaphysics, are but the physical demonstrations of what had started in the Etheric Body of Man. The remedies treat the *man* with the lower strength remedies dealing with the physical man. As you go into the thousand potency, it has been stated that you are no longer dealing with the physical but with the Etheric Body. The ten thousand and the fifty thousand potencies could very well be concerned with the

Mental and the Causal Bodies. All illnesses that manifest in the physical plane have their origins in the "other bodies", for the law follows that the manifested world reflects the unmanifested or invisible worlds. Involution preceeds evolution.

As you evolve spiritually, you must take care of the problems and the obstacles and the limitations of the physical. It is the overcoming of these problems that will open up the centers within you to allow the Higher Self to express itself more fully.

Transcendental experience confines itself to the human kingdom, for none of the other kingdoms has the power which is in mankind. Mind must be present in order to recognize the elusive Realities, and although *all* life exhibits a degree of intelligence, only the human level possesses Mind as an individual faculty. Through what is termed the "Third Eye" (Lemurian civilization aspect), Intuition, etc., you can come to the state of conscious mastery of self and have "Self-hood."

You are the only one who can open the door to transcendental experience for the faculty for it is within you. Again, no one else can do it for you. So, do not waste effort or time in pursuing the temporary, material things, but strive earnestly and sincerely for that which is real and permanent.

It is interesting to note here that when the Cosmos initiated the movement of Involution and the universes manifested, *It* automatically was limited by its own action. At one point on the evolutionary scale, the Creative Energy of the Cosmos divided itself, for its power was too great for manifestation on lower levels in its pristine essence. It could have consumed all, so the duality entered onto the scene. Part of this original energy remained, and still does, in the higher spheres or planes; the other part completed the Involution and is now involved with evolution.

Following this line of thought, remember that you are the projection of the Higher Self made manifest on the earthly plane of existence. As the Cosmos refrained from having all of itself manifested, so the Higher Self withheld part of itself. It, then, is the goal and the underlying principle of mystical experience that you re-unite yourself with the Higher Self. It is the "going to the Temple within," the Temple of your Reality, the seat of all that was, is, or ever will be. You are really but a fragment of consciousness until this unification of the outer and the inner is materialized.

Whether you reach this through the Inner (Interior) You or the Outer You is not that important, really. In the long run, you will still have to quell the dominance of attention to the five physical senses in order to live from the "heart-center". Concentration on the higher aspirations is necessary and you should contemplate on the origins of nature, of yourself and of all that is. In so doing, you will reach the Reality of your Mind, and also reunite the two segments of the essence of *you*!

Attainment to this point depends upon how successfully you detach your attentions from the sensual aspects of your life and free yourself from dwelling too much with values placed improperly on the external features, the temporary glamor of things or materiality. No effort on your part will result in further development until this is done, and you must resort to self-disciplinary measures to arrive at this particular stage of detachment.

You can best reach detachment by changing your direction of thought. Analyze and then eradicate the thoughts that give you the "false gods" of money, security, things. Realize that every thought spent on these areas are the two thieves witnessing your self-crucifixion on the "Cross of Materiality." By proper emplacement of consciousness, you can transmute the wasted thought energy into areas more constructive, more lasting, and more real.

Next, if you change your thoughts, then change your emotions or feelings into a direction which is more positive. Recall the statement, "Active calmly, calmly active," and apply this principle in as many situations as is possible. This does not mean that there is no feeling, but rather that feelings are now properly used. Replace sympathy with compassion, physical love with Divine, all-encompassing love. Do not permit emotions to reign over you; you should be the master of all of your feelings. Mystical experience cannot be, so long as you allow the emotions to run riot with you.

Your daily life should be characterized by order and with definitive purpose and understanding. Realize that all things in your life and in the lives of others have a part in the Cosmic Scheme or else those things would not be. Nothing is by chance. The proper perspective for you involves right ordination of your thoughts injected into your daily life activities. Everything that is related to everything else and to everybody, so the Oneness that pervades the Universes should be the center from which you program your daily living. Remember that the job at hand is the most important one and should be done to the best of your ability, always rightly and correctly. Your problems will reflect this new attitude, and the solutions will be readily discernable as you refine your thoughts, feelings, and actions.

Your new direction in thoughts can best be accomplished by entertaining those ideas which will create constructive and spiritual reflections. Each day, as often as possible, ponder over some of the occult teachings, the Cosmic Laws and Truths which you have learned. Enlarge your imagination to encompass the extension of Truth beyond what you already know and conceive. You "are where your mind is", so it would be advisable to concentrate or contemplate on high level thoughts which would develop your spirituality and reflect in the lives of others.

Feelings can often be transmuted immediately if you just make the effort to still yourself in moments of crisis or stress—whether in you or the environment about you. Fall into the habit of meditating—quietly and unobtrusively. In putting your consciousness on a great thought and in quieting yourself for meditation, the feelings or the emotions subside. Then, you can work at transmuting the energy of the negative emotions that were disturbing you.

It is to be kept in mind that although you turn away from your feelings momentarily, still yourself, and think metaphysically, you yet have the previously discharged energy to deal with. The former, negative emotions and the forces contained within them are in the ethers of all the planes. This is what you must transmute as well as the feelings you entertain at the moment. Your own re-directing of your thoughts, feelings, and actions are a personal alchemy, but it does not mitigate what negativisms you had been guilty of harboring. The transmutation process comes through conscious effort on your part.

Detachment and self-discipline are some of the basic aims of the yoga principles. Yoga itself involves duality, for it is, actually, a method and the results of the methods used. Too many limit the scope of yoga by considering only the physical exercises and methods involved in attaining self-mastery. It is also a mental conditioning as well, for yogis aim at unifying the Mind, the ultimate goal of the study, with the World Mind. To achieve this last condition, you must turn your attention inward, learn how to be serene and quiet by quelling all thought activity. In this way, it is hoped that the practitioner will reach deeply within and have the Cosmos and the Cosmic Pattern shown to him.

Meditation requires selecting a place and a time. When you decide on meditation as a means to develop yourself, it cannot be a sporadic effort, but you should be prepared to form the *habit* of meditation. Too often, you will resign yourself to meditation when and if you have the opportunity to do so, but this defeats your plan to develop. It really is the first step to self-discipline—establishing a daily routine for meditation. Review your day and notice how and when you can establish a period of time that will allow you to meditate consistently. It could mean that you might have to re-arrange your schedule to fit this in.

Most of you are entangled in a series of habits — a framework of routine actions carried on from day to day. This routine is not easy to break and you are, actually, a prisoner in your own jail. Replace many of the old habits with new ones — including a meditation period. With a new perspective and determination, you will be able to manage meditation each day, and no longer will you claim you are too tired, too busy. Tomorrow is too late sometimes. Do it *now*!

There are many hindrances to attaining results in meditation, which is a good method to reach mystical experiences. The usual guides of being in a quiet place, avoiding being interrupted, sitting quietly, and the pre-preparations as described in the chapter on the "Development of Psychic Powers" are essential for proper meditation in which you could have a mystical experience. However, there are other features to be observed which could be a deterrent to achieving this state of development.

Health is important, for Spirit encounters blocks to its expression and communication with you when any malfunction of the body exists. The ill health would distract attention that you need for this exercise. Still, many in ill health or a crippled condition have had unusual results in meditation that were of a mystical nature. Do not be impatient either, for results might be slow in coming and you might want to give it all up.

One never knows exactly when a mystical experience will be. It could come when observing a great painting or listening to fine music. When someone passes on who had been quite close, you might have a mystical experience. This last example occurred to me just two years ago. My army buddy, Herbert Morris, who had been more a brother to me than just a friend, had passed away rather suddenly, four years previously. At the time of the incident, I had been visiting with his wife and his sisten and went to meditate at a plaque which had been erected in his honor in the municipal building in Orange Park, Florida. The plaque had a three dimensional colored picture of Herb. In my hand, I held a watch of his; it had been lying in a box of his personal jewelry for four years and had not been touched to that date since his death.

When meditating at his picture, I concentrated on a problem for which I sought an answer. This, of course, was not the right thing to do at that time, but since it dealt with certain situations in his family, I felt that I might help if he could show me the way. Instead of an answer to the problem, I distinctly heard Herb's voice say,

"All is as you said it would be." We had spent many, many hours discussing metaphysics, and to me, this was the finest proof I could have.

When I felt that I had been there long enough, I sat down on a sofa in the lobby and, at the same time, put the watch down on the sofa also. Strangely enough, the watch which had stopped at four o'clock four years before was now running. When I related this incident to Evangeline, his wife, she assured me that the watch had never been out of the box in four years; she gave it to me. The regular time at which this had happened was 11:15 in the morning. On the plane that night (7:00 p.m.) I finally wound up the watch, which had been constantly running for eight hours!

Another incident occurred later that afternoon. His wife was so impressed by what had transpired that she asked me to conduct an experiment. She took Herb's other watch out of the same box, it too, had not been touched or wound for four years. She placed it in a plastic bag and asked me to hold it while we drove over to their old home which she had sold after Herb left. While driving to the house, entering the drive, parking under the back garage portico, and walking to the house, it started again and continued while we walked to the car and drove out of the driveway. Once out of the drive, it ceased working. I then asked Evangeline to drive two blocks away and turn around. The watch still refused to work. As soon as the car was headed back to the property, the watch commenced its movements and went through the identical procedure as before.

To me, having had many experiences in metaphysical studies and having read so much and discussed so much with others who had these experiences, it was another example of not only the continuity of consciousness (on Herb's part), but also it served as further proof of many things to me. Every now and then, we all need proof to bolster up our beliefs or our theories. Gradually our beliefs are built upon these proofs and no further ones are required, but they can come to you as needed or as examples.

Other hindrances to mystical experience exist. From certain Sutras from Tibet you can be taught the interior and exterior obstacles that exist which confront you and interfere with self-mastery. These obstacles block your path to the near perfection of the true mystic or Initiate.

These Sutras or Transmissas list eleven interior obstacles:

1. The first interior obstacle is ignorance—ignorance of the highest object of aspiration (Oneness). This condition can be remedied by your possessing right knowledge and thereby having proper direc-

tion in your life. Proper direction will give you a clarity of purpose and perspective.

2. The second interior obstacle is passion, which is carnal (lust), material (greed), spiritual (pride in a personal sense of ego-promotion). The appropriate remedies for each of these are: fortitude, temperance, prudence, and justice. Each of you should be in pursuit of that which is good through the use of personal-will.

3. The third interior obstacle is inertia. You are all creatures of habit and tend to remain as you are without making the effort to change. Change is the Law of Life; without it there is no motion, no movement forward. To overcome this obstacle requires the use of right effort coupled with right motivation.

4. The fourth interior obstacle is known as debility of will, and is overcome by self-discipline. All Cosmic Laws and Truths represent the guides or disciplines, for the application of these principles would demand the use of will—determined and sincere will.

5. The fifth interior obstacle is coldness or indifference—a result of a lack of motives. Involvement in a spiritual development would stimulate correct feeling and perspective which bring a conscious, personal relationship with you to all people and to all things.

6. The sixth interior obstacle is illusion. Time and circumstances subject you to limitations. Through the use of Mind and imagination, you are able to see the proper place of everything in the created and manifested Universe. You then afix attention on the Realities rather than the actualities.

7. The seventh interior obstacle is false perspective. This is ovecome by re-alignment of your values to the understanding of the importance or unimportance of all things. Knowledge and the application of the Cosmic Laws and Truths help you in attaining the proper perspectives.

8. The eighth interior obstacle is one-sidedness, which brings about the atrophy of your faculties and powers. Correcting this is done by open-mindedness, broader vision, higher ideals.

9. The ninth interior obstacle is small-mindedness—not grasping or refusing to accept that which might conflict with your established habits or beliefs. The Sutras tell you that this can best be conquered by developing general culture.

10. The tenth interior obstacle is limitation of outlook. Improper or incomplete knowledge limits your understanding, perspective, values. You can correct this by developing universality of knowledge.

11. The eleventh interior obstacle is limitation of sympathy. The word, "sympathy" could be much misunderstood in the sense of feeling sorry for someone. Perhaps the word, "compassion" might better be substituted. You overcome this obstacle by the use of universal love, or the feeling of Oneness with all in the manifested worlds.

These, then, are the interior obstacles which could be instrumental in delaying or prohibiting mystical experiences in your life. Added to these are the exterior obstacles. Duality becomes quite evident again with the two aspects at play in your life. Exterior obstacles are the result of the interior ones. The Transmissa on these obstacles states, "to achieve a more satisfactory, and with time a more perfect, condition in all avenues of the personal life, it should be realized where the negative activity lies, only then can negative HABITS be changed to positive ones. The energy is always available, direction is the only requirement. The most startling changes can be made in health by working on the physical body with interior methods. With a good instrument, vitality is maintained for mental or metaphysical work."

The following exterior obstacles are presented through the same Sutras from Tibet:

1. The first exterior obstacle to perfection is lack of health which is intellectual, moral, or physical. Often this can be outside of your control, in a way. Physical ill health results from wrong habits of eating, lack of exercise, improper sleep, and ignorance of physical hygiene.

Intellectual ill health, to a certain degree, depends upon your physical condition. Mental illness can be caused by physical disorders. Other mental illnesses can be overcome by proper thoughts and study with sufficient periods of retreat from the pressures of mental activities.

Moral illness is based on wrong thoughts, speech, feelings, and actions. You can best conquer this by encouraging self-mastery through the will and decreasing negative habits.

Any of these three illnesses can be avoided when you patiently and continuously strive for normalcy. All illnesses may be eliminated by correcting your mental and emotional attitudes. Wrong emotions stimulate nervous disorders. Fine, correct emotions bring good health. Eliminate worry, fears, hatreds and your health will improve.

2. The second exterior obstacle to perfection is excessive poverty. The Sutras classify poverty into three categories—absolute (very small income), relative (small income on which you can barely exist), acute (does not even have the bare necessities). Poverty can

cause you to have to pay so much attention to securing the material essentials that you do not have the time to develop yourself spiritually. Sacrifice is often necessary for those who are excessively poor. But through work, thrift, and requesting aid when needed, the situation could be alleviated. Meet your responsibilities, attempt to do all work well, and strive, with hope, for your success. Care must be taken that you do not put too much emphasis on the acquisition of wealth for the sake of itself and its possession only. This could be the greatest obstacle of all. It is also not advisable to overcome poverty through illegal or doubtful means. You can still achieve a degree of mystical experience despite poverty.

3. The third exterior obstacle to perfection is imprudent diet. Excess in eating and drinking should be avoided. There are some foods which produce psychic states which are favorable to spiritual development. Foods that will stimulate should be avoided however, and liquid stimulants as well despite the fact that some of them do promote the imaginative faculties. Especially if these things are taken in excess is it most dangerous and detrimental to you. However, the Sutras do state that, "Owing to the potency of the Spirit, it is theoretically possible to attain any desired result on the higher planes even without the aid of dieting or other physical expedients. The Initiate should be sufficiently independent of material things to be able to eat and drink with pleasure in the house of a stranger whatever is set before him; however he may regulate his own table."

4. The fourth exterior obstacle to perfection is lack of leisure. Few of you have order in your lives, and consequently, life becomes a hit and miss type of thing, with activities geared either to excessiveness or to tenseness. Little thought is given by you to the leisure time of quietness and the constructive pursuit of Truth in which you could learn and experience the mystical approach.

5. The fifth exterior obstacle to perfection is lack of sympathy from the members of your household. This is a familiar story to many of you in the field of occult metaphysics. Family members tend to be indifferent or even hostile toward your participation in the study of metaphysics. It could lead to unpleasant home situations, frustrations on your part, criticism and ridicule leveled at you. The ideal circumstances would be if all the family joined you, but this can hardly be expected. However, through the use of the Cosmic Laws and Truths, you can establish cooperation and understanding from them to you in your interests. There are disadvantages and drawbacks for you if you have to function under these oppositions

from the family members, and these could prevent development or slow it down.

6. The sixth exterior obstacle to perfection is concerned with wrong customs in your community. Often the atmosphere of a community or neighborhood could act as a deterrent to your progress. The town could be a crude area; it could be a section where bias and prejudice exist; moral order might be lax; false values might be placed on materialism, status, etc. All these would interfere with your advancement in striving for evolvement. The town could be in disorder and corruption. These are all harmful influences, and by living among them, you feel the effects. Remember that man is imitative, and it is easier to do that which is best when you are surrounded by others who are engaged in the negativisms stated. It is always most difficult to stand alone. The Sutras recommend selecting those who set a good example to be close associates. Realize your ideals and aims in life and you could have some influence upon others.

7. The seventh exterior obstacle to perfection, according to the Sutras, is that you have "to contend not only against obstacles naturally resulting from the defects of (your) environment, but also against the active opposition of those who are opposed to (your) ideals. The protagonist of the Ideal is sure to be resisted and even hated. . .Those who are ignorant of the superior importance of and value of spiritual, intellectual, moral, and aesthetic aims despise and oppose (you if you refute the) supremacy of the physical and the material."

8. The eighth exterior obstacle to perfection is the negative action taken by those who are ignorant and are preyed upon by those who espouse the cause of evil and use the ignorant to carry out the evil work.

9. The ninth exterior obstacle to perfection involves those who have intelligence but deny the existence of the Absolute and speak many invectives against you for aspiring to spirituality and Oneness with the Ultimate. While you aspire to the highest good, realize, at the same time, that even these unfortunate intelligences are being subjected to evil powers which are greater than they are.

10. The tenth obstacle to perfection is "unfavorable psychophysical or cryptic and occult influences." Anything that is negative around you and in others can act upon your soul and body. This is particulary true with marriage and with close family ties, for you are being influenced by their thoughts and emotions. "Close contact with any person. . .exposes (you) to the occult influences which

everyone exercises without knowing it." The degree to which this can effect you will depend upon your own strength and knowledge and the strength of the personality and influence of the other person over you.

MYSTICAL LIFE

Law and order are the diving pattern of the Universe. Everything bears a relationship to every other thing and to the Infinite Spirit, for we are part of the one great whole. You might not consciously perceive or realize this fact, but your ever-changing emotions and thinking continually unite you with different and various aspects of the Universe.

This is, of course, a vast concept leading into infinity, but by concentrating on this idea with high inspiration, you will reach out into the great expanse of Universal knowledge and gain much wisdom and truth. There is no limit to what might be gained through a steady vortex of sincere spiritual aspiration.

Even though you might think you are living and doing as you desire and that you are disregarding the things that do not meet with your favor, still you are being automatically and eventually propelled into Law and Order.

The atomic law of unity exists throughout the entire universe and runs through every individual as well, and you are either helping or hindering the progress of an intelligent understanding of your place in the Universal Whole. If you understand the Laws and live within them, you are helping in the evolution of the race. If you are ignorant of the Laws and live haphazardly, you are hindering and defeating your own progress and that of others also.

The Law of Oneness exists through all life. The God-Force permeates everything and everybody as a great illuminating power enfolding the entire universe. The cohesive force which unites the universe is Harmony (Love). Therefore, you realize that when you are, so to speak, out-of-love, you are out of Harmony with the Universe and hence are a discord. As civilization stands today, you can divide humanity into three main categories: the animal, the human, and the idealistic. Of course, there is no distinct dividing line among the three, but they gradually graduate out from one another and all partake, to a certain extent, of the qualities of the others. However, a certain majority of one classification will, in many, indicate to which class you might belong at the present time.

The animal classification of humanity is not meant in a derogatory sense; the term is a means of distinguishing the different stages of growth. Animals are rules primarily by instinct and have certain other qualities which have been evolved in the evolutionary pattern for their kingdom and species. Some of these qualities are those of self-defense, propagation, mother-love, industry, patience, energy. However, all of these qualities concern themselves with the bare necessities of living.

The human classification concerns those associated with the things in life which belong essentially to the race of man rather than the animals. The outstanding characteristic of these people is self-centeredness, and their lives are molded by Self rather than by instinct. The development of self-centeredness brought about certain characteristics such as self-expression and self-promotion. Therefore a display of emotion and feeling resulted. With time these people developed as creators of beauty and had power and property. The attitudes of this group towards the Ultimate or the Absolute was one of seeking more and more help. These people live for beauty, entertainment, comfort, self-expression; fundamentally, they live for themselves and for those things which contribute to their personal happiness, pleasure, and comfort. There is a mass of these of this classification, and they can be influenced either for the constructive or the negative through their emotions and feelings.

The idealistic class is comparatively new, for as yet, it encompasses a very small percentage of the world's population. Those within this group have become detached or decentralized from their own personal interests. They share their successes, works, and experiences and are very cooperative and evolved to general brotherhood of all. They recognize individual responsibility for world conditions; their feelings extend beyond the home, family, and national affiliations. Their attitude towards the Infinite is one of service and a desire to comprehend the Cosmic Pattern, Laws, and Principles.

Now that the New Age is upon you, you will discover more examples of this group. All three classes represent three human phases of evolution, referred to as Animal Consciousness, Self Consciousness, and Cosmic Consciousness. As part of the Aquarian Age, you have the opportunity of entering the third phase in which you will not be governed primarily by your emotions but will learn to control and to transmute them to higher expressions of Harmony. The God of this New Age will not be the man-made God of the past, but Truth, impersonal, all-powerful, and all-knowing, able to stand all the tests of time.

You will comprehend God as Law and Order, which is closely allied to scientific principles. Emotional living is to be supplanted by Mind.

Mind, the Higher Self, is becoming the dominant force with mankind, part of the new spiral of evolution on which you have been launched with the New Age momentum. This Mind stage is the object of the Aquarian Age, and many, especially the young, have responded to the higher vibratory rate of the age. Now is the time in which there is more interest evidenced in the higher spheres of thought and truth.

You live in a state of constantly becoming, for there is nothing stationary in nature. All is either progressing or retrograding. Because you erred in the past, you should not condemn yesterday, nor forget it entirely, for you use them as lessons for tomorrow, but above all, for today. Because of what you did yesterday, you are, or should be, wiser and stronger. You advance or regress according to your ability to absorb the lessons and experiences.

If you work harmoniously with the Law, the Law will automatically protect you as you strive for the illumination and the experience of the awakening of the Cosmic Force within you. It is only when you stimulate this latent force within you that the spiritual initiations begin and you evolve. There is this PRESENCE that you contain, like a light. At first, as you develop, there will be tiny flashes, momentary experiences, but sufficient enough to grant an idea of the grandeur of the possibilities which lie in store for you. From the first experience of this, you will find the courage, enthusiasm, and, above all, patience to continue with the effort for spiritual development.

As this continues within you with successive attempts and advancement, the Christ Consciousness (Cosmic Consciousness) begins to exhibit itself. From this moment on, you will live your life as a soul with the soul qualities predominating rather than the personality aims, desires, and feelings. You feel a sense of Unity with the Whole, and with this, comes the realization of service to all that is.

You might be prompted to ask: "How does one experience this PRESENCE and the light?" Re-evaluate yourself and see if you have attained to harmlessness in thought, word, and deed. Do you refuse to think negatively about others? Have you attained to the point where you do not pass judgment or criticize another?

Can you detach yourself from personality—yours and others?

you can honestly state that you have reached all these stages of development, you stand on the threshhold of Initiation and Illumination.

Now, the Initiation is not necessarily a defined ceremony that you go through. You will *know* when you have had the Initiation, for there will be an increased awareness and sensitivity in all of your daily experiences and to all life in all forms. You will have a greater interest in and more ability to help others, for you will reflect the PRESENCE AND THE CONSCIOUSNESS. You will have a greater realization of all things as they are and you will be in complete Harmony.

Those who do not have this evolvement are still working from the outer personality or lower selves, not from the soul center. They still observe the defects, the faults, the shortcomings of others and the world in general. To evolve, each of you must begin to see only the good that resides within all and within everything. It might be dormant good or only slightly developed good, but it is there nevertheless. When you see the good only, you assist in bringing it forth by the Law of Attraction.

Light has been defined in occult circles as knowledge. Often it is described as "fire." The source of spiritual power is this "fire", and it is for this that the Initiates of all ages have ascribed to and taught a philosophy of fire, which is the foundation of all occult law. All illumination develops when you ignite the fire of the Soul (the experience of Moses and the burning bush).

Those of you who are interested in this way of life must first discard the old, false thought patterns you have been living with and by. Do not seek the results as a phenomenal, exoterical nature. The personalities of the Masters and the Ascended Ones are not important. When you have mastered the lower self, you will encounter what you seek, but it will not necessarily be a face or a form, but of a nature that will surpass your wildest imagination. Form will not be accentuated, but the force of the "fire" or light will be overwhelming and very intense.

Do not be satisfied with where you are now, but endeavor to gain this light. Work from the soul-qualities within, not from the personality without when you deal with others and the problems of life. Personality frailness brings failures and unfortunate conditions, so you eliminate this by working from the force that is within you. When you serve, serve with detachment of the personality.

There is a great need today for channels through which the Masters can function, for they work through the Illumination of the Soul-Light or fire.

You must make changes in your thinking and feeling. You must forgive grievances and erase them from your mind and heart. The Law is automatic. If you think you have been wronged in any manner, it is because you have been guilty of wronging others, and by the Law of Attraction, similar conditions came to you.

Work for the attainment of Illumination and the birth of Cosmic (Christ) Consciousness. When you begin to achieve this, you will love unselfishly; you will observe from the soul-center; you will be attuned with and work through the Cosmic Consciousness.

Perhaps the most difficult thing to accept is that you must forget about the future rewards and the glories, for the most important aspect is in the "Now"—the job at hand being the very necessary one. Only through the every-day chores of every day living can you master the lower self and generate the energies of the Higher Self. When you advance; every faculty has to be uplifted to serve on a higher level of manifestation. Do not forget that the opposite pole of every vice and fault is a virtue into which the vice and fault might be transmuted.

The Specter and the Angel, representative of the debits and credits of your incarnations, are with you constantly. You must burn out the dross of the lower self and eliminate the defects and faults. Then, the Angel (Guardian) aspect becomes brighter and fuller while the Specter dwindles in stature and power. They are the creatures of your making, and you can master them.

First, you have to realize that MIND is something entirely different from the physical brain, infinitely greater, and that which remains with you through all eternity. Mind uses the brain as an instrument. The mind must be working properly in order to obtain the best results in your daily living, and in order to obtain this, the influence of the Higher Mind must be brought into play through the psychic and subconscious minds into the conscious every-day working part of your brains.

The Aquarian Age requires that each of you must assume a role of individual thinking so that your Higher Mind, through the Law of Attraction, will be synchronized with the minds of the Masters instead of the mass mind. Mass thinking is characterized by unruly, uncontrolled emotions.

Your important work is the conscious control and manipulation of thought. Above all things, endeavor to find Truth in a sincere manner, develop tolerance, and kindness towards your fellow man. Keep the ideal of perfection before you at all times and live your life from the source of Harmony. Realize the Oneness with all kingdoms of the earth and all the elements. When you do this, the inhabitants or forces of all the kingdoms and all levels react to your rate of vibration. To you they will turn for aid in their own evolutionary progress.

The invisible planes of life assist and guide you as your vibrations register the spiritual progress that you make. As you raise your consciousness, the atoms of your body also undergo a gradual change. Your entire body will vibrate at a higher rate, and you, in turn, become aware of other and higher states of consciousness. You will find that you are being influenced by higher forces from higher planes. Too, as your higher mind functions more and more, your psychic senses emerge from the dormant stage. This growth will be accompanied by mental development and spiritual advancement, and then, nothing is hidden from you. However, before you reach this state, you have to prove yourself worthy.

As you attune your mind to the higher minds and raise your vibrations, you are entrusted with the Laws by which the universe is governed. Your mind is then used for the reproduction of things that will aid humanity toward perfection. These Laws are never given to you if you intend them for your own material gain or self-aggrandisement.

As you are obedient to the Cosmic Laws and Truths and work in Harmony with higher forces, you are used by them for the furtherance of evolution on earth. Earth is a school of experience, a testing ground for evolving humanity. If you sincerely attempt to help others, quietly and unselfishly, the Power of the Absolute will be given to you.

Train your mind in a quiet, reverent manner in order that you can contact the Higher Forces. This contact will bring you the peace and wisdom that you seek, and you will no longer have to look for those who need your help. You will be led to them, or they will be led to you.

There are different planes of Spirit, the lower and the higher planes: the emotional plane, the mental plane, etc. In the Aquarian Age, humanity is vibrating closer to the mental plane, and it is also the purpose of this present root race to finalize the development of the mental body. All of you are gradually moving towards the Plane of the Mind, but you can hasten this by conscious, constructive thinking and emotional control. Also, in order to prepare your manger (the body) for the inflow of knowledge from the Masters, it is most necessary that you make effort and *study*!

The New Age brings with it a great influx of spiritual knowledge to the physical plane, and you can be an instrument of expression for this if you properly study. Strive earnestly and sincerely for the Truth in order to reach this goal mentioned. Learn all you can about numbers, sound particularly, color, symbology, astrology, etc., for there is great significance behind each of these studies which will grant to you a working language on the planes of the Mind.

Approach each of these studies with caution, for there are false teachers, poor teachers, fine books, poor books. Use your sense of discrimination as to who is teaching Truth and what is expressing Truth. You can tell!

Remember that you are a God in the making and as you think, so you are. Your Mind of the future will be much different when it is synchronized and uses concepts of the highest ideals and with the knowledge of true wisdom.

Destiny, tangible or intangible, has to be met from birth to death. Once you exteriorize your thoughts and feelings, you have incorporated them into your destiny and they are a part of it. Destiny, therefore, is of your own making. Through your thinking and desires, you have the means of making your destiny one of success, health, happiness or one of failure, illness, sorrow. The degree of attainment in either direction depends upon the amount of conscious effort exerted and the degree of soul-awareness developed by you.

No one of you is alike in the states and kinds of your emotional, mental, and spiritual development, for all of you started out in this earth life in different grades of learning. It is not possible for all of you to attain the same amount of evolvement in one lifetime, but each of you can make a conscious beginning now. A beginning has to make something, or the destiny becomes more and more a restricted condition.

You would be foolish to delay or to postpone your conscious beginning, for through conscious procrastination, you extend the suffering you endure in your life. Once you *know* the Truth of self-responsibility and that destiny is of your own making, you are no longer ignorant of the Law.

With the knowledge of the Law, you then have to change the direction of your thinking. When this happens, automatically, a new quality causes changes in your material life as well. The conditions around you, the experiences you encounter, the people with whom you come into contact will all have a corresponding alteration. To those who are developed to the level in which they can see your mental-atmosphere, they see the form, color, tone, and quality of your mental thoughts, for thoughts and feelings are not hidden from their "extra" sight.

Look around you and at the world in general today. The chaos and tribulations determine the type of thinking and feeling that is being exercised by the majority of people in the world. The activities witnessed in the daily life are the results of mass thinking, and thoughts follow closely upon the heels of feeling and desires that people entertain within themselves. Few realize that their thoughts, feelings, and desires are responsible for the circumstances in their lives. Payment is extracted from them in accordance with the type of thought, feeling, and desires that they have harbored. This is the Cosmic Justice which follows the Law of Compensation.

Each day, you add to your debits and credits, and all of this is carefully registered. All of what you do and think is marked in your mental aura. This can only be erased through conscious effort on your part. You have to be ready to recognize your responsibility, to face your obligations, and to control your desires. As you accomplish this, you develop a higher mental and emotional state of being which will be the level upon which you enter in a future life. This is your destiny.

Some of you might question responsibility and obligation, but do not doubt what they are in your life. The duty of the moment is the one to be taken care of immediately, for it is the result of your past desires, feelings, thoughts, and actions. As you perform the duty of the moment with either the right or wrong attitudes, you are building on the credit or debit side of life. If your feeling-sense in regard to the duty is sufficiently strong, it will bring you a coordinated line of thought from which you may extract the knowledge for self-awareness.

Use your conscience as a guide to be strong as to *how* you think, feel, and act. It acts as a balance wheel between the debit and credit sides of life. If you add, daily, to the credit side, the conscience becomes stronger and guides you more clearly. But if you pile up on the debit side with the wrong desires, feelings, and thoughts, then, conscience becomes weaker, and the Specter becomes stronger.

When you deceive others, you lose your power of discrimination, and so the liar is forced into troubles and hardships caused by his own lie-repercussions. Added to the physical ills and hardships accruing to you as you lie, be it ever so small, there is generated a mental confusion within you which often leads to physical blindness in a future life. You blur your own thinking and dim the Light of your atmosphere even though you know at the time that you are lying. Some forms of insanity, loss of memory and mental derangements are a result of the lack of Truth, Sincerity, and Candor.

Honesty begins with right-thought and right-motive in one's self, and is then expressed constructively by one's actions in dealing with others. Honesty is not a mere passive attitude; it is an active virtue. The power of the will in the practice of honesty and truthfulness develops a strong and fearless character and is a big step in the right direction of soul development.

Into everything, whether it be desire, thought, or deed, you should bring a real sense of right and harmony, for this is the secret of health and harmony in the body as well as in the mind. Knowledge in itself does not bring power or happiness. It is only when you demonstrate the knowledge in your daily living, in doing the job at hand at the moment, that knowledge becomes real power.

Duties are important always, but when you have a knowledge of the Cosmic Laws and Truths, then the duties assume a greater role as you build your destiny and future life.

When you embark on a scientific program of soul development, or the evolving of the potentials within you, make sure that you deal openly and honestly with all of your faults and failings. You really cannot disguise them or ignore them, and you cannot attain to Cosmic Consciousness by merely subliminating these negative aspects of your character. The gifts of the Cosmic Root Substance will be handed to you as you practice and work to change these aspects by transmuting them. No one can do it for you, so it is in your hands alone.

All life is really One. The highest consciousness is that of Unity in contradistinction to separateness. You as an individual are comparable to a wave or a tiny ripple in the great ocean—a tiny part of the ocean as it were, but only seemingly separate. This is the reasoning behind the high concept or tenet which declares, "Love thy neighbor and do him no injury," for to cause harm to another is to injure yourself. In the great sea of Universal Consciousness, the Law of Cause and Effect always works automatically. That which you emit from yourself to others or to life in its totality eventually returns to you, but heavier than when it left your sphere. You have to realize the tremendous importance of continually projecting only that which is good to all and to everything regardless of who or what the conditions might be. Dishonesty, untruthfulness, and insincerity are the boomerangs which return their substance to the very persons who exercised their qualities towards others.

When you open your mind to the possibilities of soul evolvement and the work that is involved with it, when you banish the sorrows, uncertainties and confusions from your consciousness, the circumstances of life are seen as they really are and are not the illusions or appearances as they indicate to you.

When many souls begin to awaken, the entire atmosphere of the planet will change. Brutality and vulgarity will disappear. This then is the reason for the responsibility for you to evolve in a spiritual manner and raise the consciousness of the entire planet.

The proper use of the knowledge of the Cosmic Laws and Truths is an automatic protection. Thought energy or the will power you employ may be used for two distinct purposes. The thinker can direct his thoughts constructively for himself and the good of humanity or he could, apparently, be utilizing this energy for his own good but to the detriment of others who become the victims of his thoughts.

However, if you live harmoniously within the Laws, nothing can influence you adversely. Your being the living example of the Laws will be the instrument of transmuting and dissipating any negative thought forms around you. When you live within the Laws of Harmony, you place yourself beyond the reach of the evil minds of those who wish to influence you destructively. Evil thoughts and the inharmonious auras of others cannot touch you in proportion to how much you have cleansed your own mind and heart of all undesirable inclinations.

When your ideals are high, your desires right, and your spiritual aspirations are coupled with right thoughts, there is given to you the full protection. "Though a thousand die at my right, yet do I stand in the midst of the battle unharmed."

It is the principle of underlying Harmony, kindness, and forgiveness that protects you against injurious influences. Keep within this Law and "It will not come nigh thee." Equilibrate yourself with the Law of Harmony, and your own Soul-Force serves as a protective shield against evil or negative energies. It is wise to remember that you can never be affected by any negativisms, regardless of their strength, unless you have a similar energy existing within your own aura. Like attracts like.

When you study occult metaphysics, you are taught how to throw a protection around yourself when you become aware of the impingement of adverse thoughts and feelings around or directed to you. This can be done on a short range basis or a long range one. In subsequent chapters, you will read about the White Light, and this is the protective force that you call upon.

Negativism does not have to be ignored, fought against or resisted. Through the Law of Harmony, transmute the negative into the positive and it will be absorbed by the positive. When you fortify the heart center and the soul with positive thought, they become potent factors against unprincipled intentions and efforts aimed at you by others. You should never consider combating others or their influences, but rather, transmute them into the finer spheres of thought.

For the past five years, I have been lecturing publicly on the field of occult metaphysics, E.S.P., U.F.O.'s, astrology, etc. In all those years, I have never had an obnoxious heckler in the audience. Oh, there has been disagreement and questions, but always on a higher level. When I am introduced, I begin with the statement that I am not there to argue the subject with anyone, merely to explain it from the experiences and studies that I have had and am willing to share these with the audience. Those in attendance must be curious and want to know something or they would not be there. I also state that I do not want or expect to convert anyone to my way of thinking. Often, someone in the audience will say that he cannot believe in what I have said. My response is that I have not asked him to do so and that it is his right to disagree.

There have been many audiences which had had a hostile aura, but before lecturing, I put out the White Light and the thoughts of Harmony between the audience and me. So far, it has always worked and always will. I especially enjoy lecturing to groups where there are men of science—mathematicians, engineers, physicists. It is most obvious, in the beginning, that they do not subscribe to any area of metaphysics. "Show me" is the typical attitude. Well, I do not show anybody anything, for proof in any of this work is individual, but I explain as much as possible what I know about the subject. So long as I am trying to be constructive and am sincere and honest, oppositions do "not come nigh me."

This can work for you no matter where you are or with whom. Regardless of location or environment, if you cultivate the qualities of constructive thinking and sincerity of purpose and use the protection of the Laws, you assist in the awakening of the soul consciousness in each individual with whom you come into contact.

If you are prone to admit to yourself that you are a failure, you open a door through which the depressing thoughts of others might enter and add this to your own vibrations, thus intensifying your thoughts and feelings about yourself. If you do not eliminate this, you invite actual failure into your life. That which gravitates to you is a result of yourself and of your own making.

By doing the very best you can with what you have where you are, you encourage and attract energies that are producers of only good. These then augment your own efforts and give you greater strength. The transcendent forces of the universe are at your disposal when you work in this fashion and with this sincere attitude. You add to the Harmony and good in your aura which, by cntact, then influences the auric fields of those around you. You become a magnet for the Cosmic Laws and Truths to work through. You are only limited by yourself.

The Cosmic Laws function only through the effects of your radiations and vibrations. If you outwardly perform good deeds while internally harboring selfish and ignoble purposes, the Cosmic Law of Cause and Effect strips you of any protection, and you reap the negativism, for the internal purposes are the force behind your superficial deeds. The Cosmic Law is impersonal, impartial, and automatic.

If you are sincerely seeking to work within the Laws, you must act rightly because you want Harmony and good in the world and in your sphere of activity. This must be a sincere desire on your part. Live in Harmony, for you realize the desireability of it. Forgive all because in the end, all is ultimate good. Seek only that which is high and constructive, for the lesser brings only temporary pleasure and gain which is not lasting.

When you purify your thinking and desires, freedom is yours, but do not imagine that this comes in a moment. You need time, patience, and effort. Think back on the long years of habitually thinking and feeling from the negative side and realize that these cannot be eradicated in a short period of time.

One of the most difficult obstacles for you to overcome is the art of forgiveness. It is not always easy to forgive those who have been instrumental in harming you, and most of the time, you can find many justifiable reasons as to why you should bear ill-feelings towards others. Think of the Cosmic Laws and Truths, and you will see the error in such rationalization.

Recall the statement to "Forgive them, for they know not what they do." Whether or not the injury is intentional or unintentional, those who cause harm to others are really in ignorance, for if they knew the Laws, they would know that it will bring repercussions to them and not, really, to you.

When you learn how to forgive, there is less concern, less frustrations, less hurt, for the art of forgiveness brings its protection to you. The awareness of this principle and its application, places you on a higher plane of existence where those thoughts and feelings of an undesirable nature do not affect you.

This freedom is not possible unless *you* free yourself from negative thoughts and desires. It requires that you live in obedience to the Law of Love and Harmony. When you become fully aware that only the positive is truly lasting, then you progress to spiritual accomplishment.

Through your failures and the resulting effects, you can locate the causes and eliminate them. Thus each and every unfavorable experience in your life will serve as a lesson from which you can benefit.

You become free and at-one-ment with the Cosmic when you achieve constructive thinking and feeling and right action under adverse and negative circumstances. Your individualized soul knows and is aware, then, of right and wrong, of good and evil. Through this awareness can come the Illumination and the Reality of Oneness.

Think of yourself as being One and Indivisible and that whatever affects you, good or bad, in one part of your being, will affect you in all other parts as well. You can attain success, health, and security by conformance to the Laws and Truths of the Cosmos.

Have you ever asked yourself the question as to "What are the things that affect and cncern you the most?"

Many of you worry about ill-health and the lack of security. Think about ill-health, and then remember that every experience you undergo, no matter how trivial, might arouse emotions which contribute to your health condition. Think this over very carefully. Experiences are either great or small to you in proportion to the kind of emotion stimulated by the experience. What is great to you might be small to another and vice versa according to the degree of your spiritual development. Much would also depend upon the equilibrium established in our soul consciousness.

Some experiences in your life arouse emotions of calmness, peace, and upliftment. Others stimulate pity and sympathy; still others, anger, fear.

Unconstructive emotions of anger and fear and worriment cause the adrenal glands to issue an excessive amount of adrenalin into the blood stream. The pancreas then pours too much glycogen, and these cause the heart to pump more rapidly so that these fluids might be distributed throughout the body. The lungs then work faster to provide the extra amount of oxygen needed. The flow of these fluids also cause a slowing down of the digestive organs. The blook forsakes the capillaries and concentrates on the main vessels, and all necessary repair work which normally would be going on is suspended. Your entire physical machine becomes choked and toxic, and the mind reduces itself to a chaotic and an unreliable state.

On the contrary, the constructive emotions tranquilize and harmonize every cell and atom in the body. These emotions permit you to work in a peaceful manner, and the body is in greater balance. This should make you realize that if you want good health, learn to control your emotions when they are wrong and not constructive. Disharmony within the body then ceases.

You can and do control all the machinery of your physical life, so why not control the machinery of your body? Use the faculty of "imagination" or what is known as "image-making." It is this imagination faculty which brings emotions to bear or any experience you have in life. Mentally, you can reject any experience that enters your world,but it is the imagination that gives the power to the happening. Through the exercise of your imagination, the power of the experience has its effect upon you. Thus, it behooves you to use the imagination wisely and correctly as to how and where you place your attentions.

Keep your attention on the Law of Love and Harmony and you have access to its power every moment. However, when you indulge in the unconstructive, you bring discord instead of Harmony. By having stepped outside of the law of right-living (and thinking and feeling), you inherit disharmony, ill health, and no success.

When you discover that you are caught in a mesh of many unconstructive emotions or wrong-thinking, stop yourself and seek the Higher Self within you. Its good is inherent within you. You can dictate to the Higher Self and call upon the faculty of imagination for aid. Actually implant constructive thoughts into the Higher Self and encourage the imagination along the same lines.

All of this must be accomplished quietly and silently by you. Initiate the energy of the constructive thought, but then, do not discuss it with anyone. This is considered a "must" in the occult world. When you talk about something too much to others, you expend the energy and dissipate it. Also, you are keeping your attention on it, and so long as you do this, it remains within your orb, and the Cosmic cannot work on it.

During each day's experiences question your reaction to the happenings to see if they are constructive and would you wish to have your feelings and thoughts recorded permanently. Whether the reactions are good or not-so-good, use your imagination. If the reaction to the experiences of the day are good, let the imagination dwell upon the pleasantness of it. If not good, use the imagination to switch your reactions to something pleasant and constructive. In time, the imagination becomes trained to immediately seek the positive, listening to the symphonic harmony of Spirit. Then, you eliminate the discordant tones of hate, fear, worry, jealousy.

By repeating this often enough, it becomes a habit, and you will no longer indulge in dustructive moods. You will stand off to one side and objectively view yourself and your reactions to the affairs of everyday experiences. Self-analyzation will take place, and thus you rectify the mistakes and re-direct your thinking and feeling.

No one can do this except yourself, and you will know that it is not easy, but when you think about it, anything worthwhile is never easy.

Try to remember that your desires are the great power or motive force which acts as the directing element in your life. Then, it can be the "desire" for health and security that will assist in guiding you in controlling thoughts and emotions.

All life is a tremendous experience and adventure in which joy and sorrow, harmony and suffering have their appointed places. You are in affinity with all planes of life, from the lowest to the highest. The Law of Cause and Effect works in perfect fashion and all things work together for good.

Thus, your life becomes a testing ground for your quality, capacity, and character. By your daily reactions to events, you either have a fuller, richer life or a lesser, more disappointing one. It is far better for you to learn as much Truth as possible, gaining more understanding, and thus, profiting from life.

All of life, regardless of the form used, is governed by law, and there is no escape from this.

Harmony and balance are the cohesive forces of the Universe. In order to experience this Harmony and balance, you must arrive at some degree of spiritual development and thus have Harmony and balance in living. Sooner or later, according to the degree of effort made, you will reach upliftment (Cosmic Consciousness).

This upliftment might come to you at any moment in your passage through the physical plane. It might exhibit itself in daily events; it might appear during a period of happiness or a period of sorrow.

In all probability, in the lower creatures this inexpressible something must be felt as an urge, a hunger, or a dream, but in you, as a member of the human race, it is an ache for a happiness that the physical satisfactions cannot render to you. When, at rare times, you do experience this upliftment, it must be that you have raised your vibrations and touched upon the higher realms wherein the essence of Spirit dwells. You know that Spirit permeates everything and interpenetrates the higher planes.

Most of the time, if you have this upliftment or Cosmic Consciousness, it will appear, apparently, as an accident. Even if it seems to be accidental, it implies and indicates that you have been working with the Laws. Some of you can achieve this even though you do not know the Laws, but you have been working with them, cognizant of the fact or not.

You can, through study and application of the knowledge, develop your own spiritual evolvement and project your own consciousness into the higher realms and become One with the great Absolute. It is in the knowing and applying of the Laws that the spiritual growth takes place, and with it, the accompanying development of the psychic faculties.

You have to reach and retain the stage of the Stillness Within, which brings an equilibrium of the spiritual and the physical worlds. When the Stillness Within is attained, it carries with it the responsibility of still performing in the world of physical activity.

Generally, the masses allow the body to master them. The spirit within these cannot manifest clearly. Through the development of spiritual consciousness, you can become the master of your body. One author once stated that: "You are not the body. The body is merely yours to use as a vehicle."

When spiritual evolvement comes, the operating Spirit sends a strong force of light into the physical body. This comes from the etheric plane and lights up your aura, so that those with whom you contact can notice the development within you by your attitudes, your reactions to life and to people. You will radiate the qualities of Harmony and peace. This stage attracts Higher Forces on higher planes who assist you. They come to you as you indicate your readiness by the "light that shines" from you.

Most people view the Law of Cause and Effect, which is Karma as a punishment brought upon mankind. You know that it is really an opportunity or steps by which you learn Truth. Karma can be considered the challenges in life through which you learn the lessons for which you came into this incarnation—a sort of fulfillment chance. It all refers back to the old saying from the BIBLE—"As ye sow, so shall ye reap." You make your destiny.

How you react to the occurrences of your days determines whether you merit benefit or chastisement. According to the seeds planted into the ground of your environment, your harvest returns as either fine or poor. So, with this realization, you accept whatever enters into your world—hardship, sorrow, success, or happiness—for when rightly experienced, they prove to be the lessons you need for further spiritual development and the mitigation of Karma.

Every time you are guilty of an unkindness in thought, word, or action, you create Karma or an effect which returns to you sometime in this life or another.

The purpose of the Law of Cause and Effect is to make you feel the outcomes or results of your own faults and shortcomings or the results of your strengths, for Cause and Effect is both positive and negative (Law of Duality). Through the opposite ends of the polarity of life, you can learn the understanding through these lessons.

The Golden Rule of "Do unto others as you would have others do unto you" works steadily and irrevocably for the object of awakening in each individual soul the realization of the Perfect Life which has its home in the essence of pure Spirit.

As stated before, Karma is both positive and negative. The good or positive Karma results in success and happiness and a realization of the spiritual Oneness of the Universe. The negative Karma is usually a result of a lack of harmony or wisdom or ignorance. However, there is innocent ignorance and willful ignorance. When you are willfully insisting on thinking and doing things that are wrong, you are willfully ignorant, but the motive behind it all determines the Karma. The one who commits wrong because of being a member of a society which contains false concepts of behavior or just does not *know* he is committing a wrong, is, of course, innocently ignorant.

It is up to each of you to recognize mistakes and misdoings and make the effort to correct them in every way.

Just remember that as you continue with your daily lessons in living that every experience of whatever degree is an expression of the Infinite, and all of it you have earned.

The Inexpressible Something beyond, perhaps, your present ability to understand, grants the happiness to all the relationships that you have. Contact with this Force is only found at a certain point on the path of experience, and when this happens to you, you will know that you know, but it will be an individual happening.

This Inexpressible something is often referred to as the internal Kingdom of Heaven, the domain of your interior forces, capacities, and capabilities with which you are endowed, and these are only *limited by yourself*, your inertia, or your unwillingness to fulfill the obligations of the Law. In order to fulfill the Law, you have to search within (Christ said, "Go to the Temple within") and attain its mastery.

It is your heritage to succeed, have happiness and peace in all departments of your life. Attainment here to any perceptible degree is conditioned by how completely you live, feel, and think within the Law.

The Law of Exchange states that you must give in order to receive, and if you accept, you must return in like value, either in material things or in service. Most people in life attempt to ignore this Law, taking as much as they can out of their daily living and giving little in return. By trying to get something for nothing, they merely destroy themselves.

If your life seems unsuccessful, cluttered up with non-essentials and the trivia of the mundane world, you have misdirected yourself from the soul's viewpoint. Somewhere along the line, you have not met your obligations to yourself and to others and have not met the requirements necessary for success.

Since you are part of the Cosmic Substance, you possess all the attributes, potentialities, and powers of the Absolute. So, if you have failed along the path, it is because of ignorance or the misuse of your powers, abilities, and knowledge. The Inner Power is within, not something external to you, and it is not dependent upon external forces. Seek the guidance within you and not try to find it on the outside.

You will discover that it is very practical to search for success within your own soul. You have only to make the effort, open the door, and work in order to prove the strength of this Truth. Daily use of these Laws will prove their value. They bring, too, knowledge and understanding to you. While in the flesh, it is your responsibility to learn and to progress. After the transition of the physical body in what is commonly known as "death," you then assimilate the effects of your present incarnation.

Learn the Cosmic Laws NOW!! Learn to live, think, feel correctly and all things will then be added to you.

This Kingdom of Heaven within you pertains to the spiritual and the material worlds. Each of you must find it for himself and live from the soul awareness. You have to establish a pattern of soul unfoldment and bring the latent forces to a state of dynamic efficiency. If you readily accept this personal responsibility and exert all effort possible, you will realize that all things are within and very available and most productive for you.

Negativisms are not based on spiritual reality, for they are primarily based on wrong beliefs and opinions. All energy is the Infinite, but you qualify or condition it with the negative aspects, send it out, and reap the result according to kind.

Your soul awareness demands honesty, sincerity. Know your

faults and transmute them. Your cruelties, tempers, etc., are the remnants of the animal traits still within your physical senses. Constantly review and analyse yourself daily to check these left-over traits. Sublimate these tendencies and control your negative impulses.

You know yourself only through the development of the soul awareness and through illumination. This adds stability to your character, restlessness and uncertainty disappear.

The idea of sublimating desires and impulses requires a bit of caution. You must ascertain that the lower self desires are truly sublimated and that it is not an oblique indulgence of the lower senses as is often witnessed in religious mysticism and in phenomena. Your true power rests not in instinctive emotion, but in balanced emotion expressed so that your entire being is harmonized and works toward evolvement—of yourself and of humanity. You have to have soul understanding; you must work; you must be of service.

Through it all, you must stand in the midst of the mundane world and this work is harmony. Harmony is achieved only by realizing that all are One and that all are your brothers, regardless of nationality, color, or creed.

Spirit, of itself, is not personal or individual; it is an essence and possesses all the attributes and potentialities of the Cosmos or the Creator. To awaken this essence, the mind has to recognize and be aware of the Soul Concept.

Looking for the Kingdom of Heaven within you is a twofold effort and process. It must include the development of the faculties and possibilities latent within your soul, and it must embrace the purification of your desires and motives to assure the correct use of those powers for Harmony with the Law. Remember that it is your responsibility to accomplish this—"Only the laborer is worthy of his hire—(after he had labored)."

You are where you are meant to be because you put yourself there. Where you are and what you are doing shows that a lesson is to be learned, a debt to be paid. Complaining about it all or doing nothing will not lift you out of the position you are in right now. You have to be willing to make the effort to free yourself from the things that bind you, remembering that your chains are of your own forging. Do not think that circumstances, other people, or things are retarding your progress in the development of your spirituality. Be determined to overcome all the limitations in your life; make a constant effort and you will find the Oneness and the Harmony of life.

If you do this, the new life you lead will be a richer, fuller life.

Very little of value or benefit from your past life will be lost, but you will see each problem in a different perspective and understand all things. Certain things in your present life will go because you have altered the direction of your desires, but those things that will go from your life will be supplanted by greater things with more value and more meaning to your spiritual progress.

THE WAY TO TRUTH

All of you are seeking a way to the ultimate truth, but the problem which confronts each of you is how and where the path to Truth is to be found. Basically, of course, it is discovered through knowledge and ALL knowledge is based on experience. You can, eventually, find THE way to Truth, but this will depend largely upon how much you love, forgive, weep. laugh, work, and serve through your experiences gleaned in your life's journey. The ultimate arrival at Truth is reached when you consistently apply your energies to life and study deeply into the mysteries of life itself. Because it requires sacrifice and devoted service, you must remain firm and you experience the trials and tests which come to you. All of those who have ascended and attained ultimate Truth have suffered, have felt the nails of Cause and Effect (Karma), and have known and shed tears of loss and sorrow. Still, they learn that in order to attain to Truth, there had to be sincereity of effort, humility, and detachment from the non-essentials of life.

One hears much about detachment, but how do you go about attaining this? Detachment is the most difficult for you to attain, for we are geared to a society which emphasizes "things". Attention rivits itself on money, homes, cars, position (not a "thing", but part of the glamor structure of society), and people. Pause a moment. Ask yourself, "Are these things really essential or lasting?" In the final analysis of life, what is reality?

Shortly after World War II, I concentrated my efforts on achieving "success"—economically, for terms of success then, and perhaps now, were thought of in money and position. Security meant a great deal to me, so I strove to establish it in life. Psychologists would, undoubtedly, attribute this to the poverty days of my childhood. Frankly, I look upon it as an alibi for my poor sense of values.

Within a few years, having acquired much of the material possessions, I took stock of myself and of my belongings. Suddenly, the "things" meant nothing, and my life lay exposed before me as a vaccuum, an empty void. What dad I, actually, achieved? Nothing really, for all that I had was subject to loss, change, destruction.

From that moment on, I stopped thinking in terms of the material things, of security, and of position. I lived my days and years as best I could with what I had, where I was. Using the occult laws and principles (making many errors and stumbling frequently), I soon discovered that I had more "things", opportunities, security, and position than I had ever dreamed possible. The focus of my attention was on the reality of life, gaining spiritual knowledge, sacrificing, withstanding the "slings and arrows." Today, I find that my "cup runneth over."

Many of you could arrive, perhaps, at this stage when it confines itself to the material appurtenances of life, but how about people? Can you face the loss of someone cherished through death or geographic distance? This is not easy, but it must be faced sooner or later. We cannot hold on to anything in this life, be it a possession or someone we love. Sooner or later, the separation takes place, so we should be prepared for this.

I recall the night of April 5, 1954, when the lady who was more a mother to me than my own, made her transition from the physical. Her daughter and I were on opposite sides of the bed, and when the last breath was taken, we looked at each other and said, "She's free at last." Then we went downstairs, told the family members, and had coffee. Less than two days later, we were all attending the first of the Cineramas in New York City. Think this is cold? No, not at all. We all had great love and compassion for the deceased one, but her teachings had shown us that you do not hold on—you must let go so that each individual soul can ascend higher. And, after all, it was only the flesh, the "mortal coil" that was left behind. Since life is continuous, the soul, mind, and personality of that very wonderful person continued and still does, and we shall all, in some higher state of consciousness be together.

When you are launched on a path which will bring you, sooner or later, to the goal of Truth, it is essential that you realize that the path is not an easy one but is often pregnant with sorrow and suffering, loss and despair. The approach on this way is not so much an idealistic one so much as one of application of effort. In the AUTOBIOGRAPHY OF A YOGI, Yogananda states, "Spiritual progress depends upon the effort made (now)." Also, you must discard the fallacy of thinking that by striving for Cosmic attainment, you become exempt from some experiences in life. *All* experiences in life are necessary for complete growth, and growth must be complete. Striving for Truth does not eliminate exposure to the depths of life or escape from the criticism of your fellow man. In actuality, when you reach a certain stage in your evolvement, you will find that all of the seemingly negative forces in life are transmuted. This is, in reality, a personal alchemy which takes place—the true alchemy which the ancient alchemists sought—the lifting of the baser materials (lower, physical self) to a higher plane of existence.

When you walk on the way to Truth, you will become aware of the fact that the tests are stronger, the temptations more potent. It is as if all the forces of the lower, physical plane have combined their energies to dominate you. In striving to evolve spiritually, you become a testing ground, and often fail, for it is here that "many are called, but few are chosen," despite the fact that they might have been shown glimpses of the Universal or Cosmic Mind and Truth. If you fail here, it will take many reincarnations before Truth is once more presented to you. It is not an easy way, but in the long run, you will discover that the hard way *is* the wasy way.

However, the hard way has results and the easy way does not. Experiences might be hard task masters when viewed on the basis of a twenty-four hour living, but from the totality of life, it is not. It follows a cyclic pattern and reverses itself, for what you do today might be hard, but ten years later, it, actually, was easy. This is because it provided the foundation of the experience for the later years. The results are seen in the later years.

When you are made aware of Cosmic Law, try to apply it in your everyday living. Immediately, the opposing negative elements will impinge upon you and your activities. These represent the test or temptations. Can you remain "active calmly, and calmy active" in the midst of a family crisis or a neighborhood fued? By remaining steadfast to the principle, regardless of the confusion around you, it will "not come nigh thee." Read the 91st Psalm and *know* that it works if you *try* it.

What do you do when someone has been unfairly criticial or has viciously made statements concerning your character or has twisted something you said? (How often this happens in all of your lives.) The first reaction might be to become angry, to go after the person, to "have it out." What does this accomplish? Nothing. By so doing, you only add fuel to the fire. So long as *you* know that you are right, forget it; bless the individual and go on your way. How difficult this is, yet how easy in the long run, for by remaining calm and working calmly, you remain well and happy. The others get themselves worked up emotionally, become ill, and are, basically, unhappy people. Too, your calmness could help them improve.

Several years ago, a local man and his wife decided to separate. The woman began accusing him and his friends of all sorts of misbehavior. For a time, those to whom she talked tended to believe her and looked with disfavor upon the husband and his friends, who were not guilty of anything she accused them. The husband and the friends kept calm, said nothing, and within four months, people were beginning to question the wife's attitudes and character. Soon, she found that she had no audience for her complaints and criticisms.

Try it, for it really works!

Too, you will find that the path to the Truth is a lonely struggle, for the Cosmic Law always prevails in that each of you must fight the "Battle of Armageddon" within yourself. There is no escape from this. So, you cannot expect an easy way to Truth, but rather that a difficult and vigorous endourance will be required of you.

On the Akashic Record is engraved all that you think, feel, and do. This Record represents all of time from the descent of Spirit into matter through the eons of incarnations, marking the spiritual evolvement or regression of your individualized spark of Spirit (Soul).

By aspiring to attain the goal mentioned, you must, first of all, have faith and hope. When you have these, you find that hope becomes faith and faith becomes reality. But how do you apply faith and hope in life? It is confined to spiritual and religious aspects, or can it manifest in the material, the everyday happenings and desires? When you know that the Cosmic Supply is constantly available to all who need it and have the faith that it can be theirs, it does demonstrate to you.

In 1959, I was returning from Mexico City and had two sons of friends of mine traveling to New Jersey for a month's visit. I had invited them for the month and so was prepared to treat them to the trip. I had estimated the cost of food and other expenses for the three of us and had provided myself with the necessary funds. For the car, I had a credit card. When we crossed the border into Laredo, Texas, I filled up the tank with gas, and we proceeded on our way.

About four hours later, I stopped for gas and discovered that I had left the credit card at the gas station in Laredo. The money I had would now have to be used for gas; we would be eating lightly, sleeping in the car, and driving twenty-four hours a day.

The car was a 1959 Bonneville Pontiace, good on gas milage, but I knew that it would be a "touch and go" situation for us. Nobody cashes personal checks for travelers—although I did try, but failed to convince anyone that my checks would not bounce. I never drove more than four hours on a filled tank. In Virginia, near Washington, D.C., I filled the tank for the last time. We arrived at the Delaware Bridge two and a half hours later, had enough money to cross the bridge and go *one* exit on the New Jersey Turnpike. The tank registered half full.

Frankly, I became slightly concerned, for going through all the little towns with their traffic and lights would consume gas quickly. Then, I realized how foolish I was. When the time came, something would happen to provide us with the means. So, I forgot about it. Of course, I took out a little insurance by sending out the thought of need to the Cosmic.

Well, it happened. Three hours later, I arrived in Pompton Lakes—the tank registered one-half full! I had, actually, travelled five and a half hours and still had half a tank of gas! Strange? Unusual? Yes, it is unless you *know* that the Cosmic Law of Supply works. Oh, I checked as soon as I arrived home. I had the tank re-filled, and it only required half a tank. The gas gauge had worked perfectly to that time and ever afterwards, so that argument was eliminated. The Mexican boys were rather shaken by the ex-perience, by the way.

How can one explain this to others? It was an individual ex-perience and proof to me. Each of you has to have his own personal experience and proof of the working of the Laws, but faith is the basic ingredient for its functioning.

Another example of faith in the Cosmic Supply demonstrated to the group of people who meet at my home to study and discuss metaphysics. Over the years, we had gathered much material and sorely needed a filing cabinet. Someone suggested that we pur-chase one, but I said that we should wait. Somewhere, someone had a filing cabinet that would come to us. Naturally, some laughed despite knowing the Laws. But, I remained adamant—a filing cabinet would come our way.

About six weeks later, a family in Pompton Lakes moved to Arizona, and the lady asked me if I could use a four-drawer, steel filing cabinet. That was the first. A few months later, a local physi-cian died, and his widow sold the home and distributed many items wherever she felt the things could be used. She contacted me and asked if I could use filing cabinets (three of them). Two other cabinets came our way within the year. Our group now uses three cabinets, and the others have been distributed where a need existed. Frankly, we were being over-cabineted, and I had to put out the thought that we had enough.

One item which should be remembered by each of you. If you need something and really and truly want it, it can be yours! There are two factors involved, however. Perhaps what you want is not really necessary, or you have not earned it in life. Always preface any desire or need with the thoughts that "if I have earned it" and *always*, "Not my will, but Thine be done." Learn the Law of Acceptance here.

The other factor to consider is whether or not you can assume the responsibilities which accompany having desires fulfilled. What you receive, you must wisely use in service to others, not selfishly. Want a million dollars? You can have it, but are you prepared for the care of it? How would you use it? The Law of Compensation is at work at all times, and if you do not earn something or misuse it in the bargain, you will lose it. Payment might be on the deferred basis, also—if not in this lifetime, then it will be made in another, but rest assured, it *will* be made.

Some might entertain the idea that all is to be had merely for the asking. Do not forget that effort must be made on your part. Nothing is being handed out by the Cosmic in an indiscriminate manner, for the Law reads, "Application of effort."

Too, many of you have probably wanted something but never seem to obtain it. Could it be that it is constantly on your mind and in your heart? In knowing the working of the Law, follow this procedure: Request of the Cosmic what you need, but then, let it go! Do not keep it on your mind, for the Cosmic cannot work on it so long as you hold it within your own sphere. Let it go and forget about it. If it comes, fine; if not, accept that it was "not meant to be." Have faith that each can receive his just share when he needs it, and it will be so. Faith can become reality.

You must, also, constantly be studying each Cosmic Law until it becomes a living part of you, so much so that you are the example, "The Word made flesh." This is the Word, and the Word is Law. The Cosmic forces will give the keys to the Truth to you if you thus study and apply the laws in your daily experiences. It must be here noted that not a single mandate or direction can be ignored, for each instruction is instrumental in your spiritual evolvement. So, again, the way is not the easy way—all Laws must be observed and put into practice.

You should not imagine either that you can pause along the way; yours must be the constant effort with rewards or harvesting as you proceed. Once committed to it, you cannot play along the way. It is not a sporadic attempt, but a constant awareness and a steady application. The Cosmic does *not* select you, the individual;

you signify your readiness by your sincerity of effort and your humility. Once you have so stepped forth, the door to Cosmic Truth, Understanding, and Power is opened to you, but you will know that it will require work, service, and obedience to all that is presented by the Cosmic Forces. Do not think otherwise, for unless there is the application of the Laws and the Truths in everyday life, all will result in failure. When following the Laws, you can meet the mundane world and recognize that everything in the manifested world is part of you. There is always assistance in this, for as you walk along the path, Cosmic Power and many of the Ascended Masters render help and guidance. All the wisdom of creation is placed at your disposal; all questions are resolved concerning the soul. All this, and more, are for each of you. "When the student is ready, the teacher appears."

It is quite fashionable today among the seekers of Truth to claim to have a Master or a Guru instructing them. I sincerely doubt that there are as many Gurus available as the number of those claiming to be under the guidance of them. People become quite confused, for the word "teacher" implies a personality, a being. This is not necessarily true for those seeking the way to spiritual development. By the Law of Attraction, when you are ready, and the Cosmic knows fully your status at all times, a "teacher" will appear. However, it can be in the form of a book, a person, or a group.

A true "Guru" or teacher does not proselyte—go out seeking followers, for the Law forbids this. When you, the student, are ready, all things will fall into place in guiding you to your "teacher"—again, a book, a person, or a group. You will know when it happens.

In metaphysical studies, the rose and the lotus have always represented the unfoldment of the spiritual forces (psychic centers or Chakras) within each person. As the rose and the lotus open to the external world, each petal appears to unfold, presenting itself to the outside world. Within each of you are psychic centers (the Chakras) which are similar to the rose and the lotus in that they must unfold and show themselves to the manifested universe. Each unfoldment signifies that one more step has been attained on the way to Truth, the ultimate goal of which is the center (of the flower and of your psychic centers) which when exposed represents the final unfoldment. However, it is still the individual's responsiblity to unfold each petal or psychic center, never forgetting that within each step of evolvement, each unfoldment lies all the WAY.

Each of the psychic centers is but one section of the totality of unfoldment. Too, some of the centers are more important than others, but nevertheless, each, as the rose and the lotus, must fulfill the pattern of unfoldment. This is accomplished by involvement in the world of matter—the world of living experiences. The centers will open up and evolve only when each man applies and obeys the Laws of Application. Those who wish to develop the psychic centers have to observe this obedience to the Cosmic Laws and the Law of Application. The Law of Application specifies that mere knowledge of the Cosmic Laws is insufficient. Each law or principle must be applied in the routine affairs of daily life. When this is done consistently, you become an example of the Law.

Despite any environmental factors which appear as obstacles to development, you can, by using every tool taught, open and revolve these centers, but, again, it is through faith and obedience to the Laws. In the center of all the psychic centers is the heart, the seat of the Seed Atom the "sanctum sanctorum", and it is through the heart center that all centers stir and function in harmony, and the soul finds mastership and is free. This is the transmutation that takes place, and all previous limitations cease to exist. When you arrive at this stage of evolvement, you feel, see, know, and strive for humanity in a conscious awareness and illumination in all your centers.

Now, you might feel that this is too ambitious and an unrealizable goal, a remote possibility beyond the realms of practical attainment. The Akashic Records state: "He who perseveres, obeys, and strives in the darkness of life, in the hurry and bustle of apparently endless obstacles, he who goes within, determined to win, no matter if starting far behind those more gifted on the wisdom path, he shall be first, and those even by right of incarnations may be the last." When you strive for the Truth, only application and steady sacrifice count. Spiritual unfoldment, the gift of the Father to His Son to possess or reject, is attained by conscious effort (will) and desire (heart), by diligent effort and the determination to complete the endeavor. Each idividualized spark in the sea of universality must eventually make this conscious effort—somewhere, sometime. This precludes passivity or neglecting some of the necessary experiences; passivity or neglect does not bring results regardless of how advanced one might have been in the past. Only by the obedience to the Law of Application can the experiences of many incarnations bring development and growth.

In order to accomplish this spiritual unfoldment, it is necessary, first, that you must look within yourself. You have to ask yourself, "Am I sincerely seeking Truth or am I merely intellectually curious? Am I attracted to it because it is different? Review your past living and determine to what degree you have suffered, to what degree you have expressed harmony (love), to what degree have you sacrificed and given to others. Too, decide how much you attempted to abide by the Cosmic Laws, how much real effort was made with faith and hope. When aware of the opening of the psychic centers, did you try to live from within these centers? Did you censure the transgressors, or did you encompass them with compassion, feeling them as your brothers?

Remember that it is not within your domain to pass judgment on others; you should focus your attention on your own failings and less upon those of others. The more attention you give to another's weaknesses, the less time and energy you devote to your own evolvement. You are a universe within yourself, and this universe of yours requires your fullest attention if it is to operate properly.

We do not mean by this that you are not to be concerned with others and their evolvement. Everything in creation influences and effects everything else. However, as you evolve, by examples you help each member of all the kingdoms to evolve. As you reflect the Truth of the Cosmic Laws, you establish a pattern or goal for others to follow. "As above, so below."

Too, evolvement varies in speed and level; there are many levels, and each of you is on your own level of development. Because you might be a little more advanced does not grant you the right to look down upon those less fortunate. There are others *above* you, and as they shed their rays to assist you, so shed your rays to others further down the ladder.

Above all, you have to decide whether the metaphysical path to Truth is actually what you want or do not want for your life.

Once you determine to face yourself and decide to follow the path to Truth, you must remain steadfast in it. You become an Initiate (one who has spiritualized the physical and is ready for the higher teachings), but only after you have withstood much, failed occasionally or many times, and have been nailed on the cross of spiritual unfoldment through the experiences in the physical realm. The Akashic Records also tell mankind that if one wishes to, he can meet the Masters but to reach this requires the complete treatment of experiences, no wasting of time along the way, and no alibis or excuses for the delays. Upon reflection, to attain all this, realize that the easy way, after all, is the *hard way*. If desiring attainment quickly, you have to learn obedience and more obedience. You have only to remember that everything given to you to do has purpose and direction, whether it be difficult or trivial. "The job at Hand" and the fact that "you are where you are meant to be" should be a guide in the realization that everything in the universe has purpose and is necessary to the development of the psychic centers. There is no such thing as "luck" or "chance"; everything falls into the Cosmic Scheme. It remains for you to learn its intent in your own life.

Once you have placed yourself on the way to Truth, you can detect the gradual appearance or manifestation of all that you have sought. The ancient teachings tell us that when you arrive at the point where the Cosmic demonstrates its Laws, you reach the stage in which the Akashic Records are open to you, and you can read the history of all your incarnations. Here it is that you confront your past, present, and future—the three are one. But to come to this stage of evolvement means obedience and faithful adherence to the disciplines of the Laws. Otherwise, you cannot read a single page from the Record. But faith and steady application of the Laws will permit you to read, eventually, these records. If your psychic centers are not opened properly and revolving at the right rate, you will not be able to focus attention on the Records. This comes about gradually through a steady progression as a result of your daily application of the Laws. Everything depends upon the effort, the sincerity within the desire.

Let it be understood, also, that no one but you, the individual, can read your particular Record. The Records are not open for all to see—just the ones who have arrived at the stage in spiritual unfoldment wherein the Record is made available. It is not done en masse or through any single agent, psychic or otherwise, but solely through the individual's own attainment. There are those who claim to be able to read the Akashic Records for others (at quite a fee) but who is to prove that what they claim *is* the Record. Only the individual will know, for any proof in this study is individual. Be cautious of those who claim to have the power to read the Book of Records, for the Law does not permit the indiscriminate reading or dispensing of the Records.

Arriving at this point in your development which involves the Records, you will possess the realization of your relationship with all in your sphere of activity and influence. The sum total of your Karma stands before you, all cause and effect pass in review. Then you fully know not only your past, but also your probable future and what you will do if you remain steadfast in your search for Truth. No further progress can be made until you, at this point in evolvement, read your Akashic Record, for greater spiritual unfoldment requires that the Initiate knows his incarnations on the wheel of birth.

As stated before, to arrive at this point in the evolutionary process requires sincere effort and application of Truth in your daily life. Through this action, you can approach this stage in your development. Every item on the list of knowledge must be thoroughly learned and used. None of this, of course, is inflexibly standardized, for all is subject to the Law of Change, which declares that change is the Law of the Universe; nothing is static or crystallized. Forms are only the vehicles through which the life (energy) expresses itself. Matter is always becoming. It is not a static universe, for whatever does not grow and expand, dies. Lack of growth means decay and death.

Regardless of how advanced you might be, free will and the exercise thereof can alter everything. Nor do you necessarily have to go further. Despite any delaying decision, however, you will eventually proceed, for the Divine destiny, man's heritage, is never lost. Mystics through the ages have taught that all will someday transmute their mistakes and reach some awareness.

In the room of the great Records is stored the vast knowledge that man has ever sought. Through this being made available, you are enabled to increase awareness and to use love, understanding, and mercy. You comprehend your place in the Cosmic Scheme, the sum total of your efforts, and how to best continue in service "doing your Father's (Cosmic) work." At this time, the means are shown and given to you in order to correlate the Time concepts of present, past, and future, realizing, finally, that one is all and all is one. Just the possibility of knowing all this is available to you should stimulate and spur you on to greater effort.

However, before you attain to Truth, you learn that you must share knowledge and experiences with others—"the cup runneth over." Anything that you learn must be applied to life so that all the kingdoms—lower and higher—can benefit and enhance their evolutionary possibilities. There is a Cosmic Law that states, "One must lose all to find all." This implies that when you arrive at the Truth, it does not relieve you, in any way, of the responsibilities and involvements in the mundane world. In fact it brings the added necessity of propelling yourself into worldy affairs to contribute your knowledge in service to the less fortunate ones, to all the kingdoms, to assist those who have transgressed and fallen by the wayside through temptation. You cannot ignore the needs of those who are suffering, for the individual's awareness of at-one-ment with all the manifested creation brings a compassionate realization of the problems and necessary growing experiences of all.

To reach a peak of evolvement and to catch a glimpse of the

Universal Truth and yet be immersed in the worldly affairs is a test. In many of the religions of the world and among some who pursue the occult, there are orders or groups that withdraw from the world and its problems. They seek spirituality, but selfishly, for the Law requires that what has been granted to you must be shared with all. Of what value is awareness if you do not move among mankind, reflecting his state for all to see and to follow? If you achieve TRUE COSMIC CONSCIOUSNESS, you know and are shown by the nature of your evolvement that involvement in worldly matters is mandatory. This very Law attests the validity of those who claim that they have arrived at this point in spiritual evolution.

Spiritual evolvement does not absolve you from assisting those less evolved and still climbing the difficult heights. This is a dangerous one for you as an evolved person, for your greater advancement depends upon your involvement in the world, your application of the Cosmic Laws, and your feelings towards those less fortunate than you. It is not easy, for to arrive so far and yet return to the mundane world can seem to be disheartening. A selfish person might just attempt to surge ahead, ignoring all those left behind who are still struggling. This is a time of decision and upon it lie the threads of success or failure for you. Very few pass this last examination, for it requires forsaking the peaks of attainment and returning to the trials and tribulations of mankind. Still, remember that the Law never fails to function, and "to lose all, one finds all." By giving a helping hand to others, by self-sacrificing, illumination becomes the reward.

The question now arises as to how much help and when should help be given to others. Often, people get caried away with their enthusiasm of what they have received in Truth and wish to impart this to others. In itself, this is fine, for you should share your knowledge and experiences with others, but it is highly questionable that this be done with everyone, everywhere.

The occult teachings stress the Law of Silence. Keep still about what you know and what you have experienced. Wait for a question to be asked in a conversation or a statement made which can guide the topics discussed along the lines of probing into life's mysteries, or a person will request your assistance. Only upon these occasions it is wise to expound the information.

I recall an incident of many years ago which adequately explains this. Several of us were invited to dinner by a family whose parents had arrived from a foreign country. The two friends with me were enthusiastic Rosicrucians and eagerly dispensed to all what they had gleaned from their studies. For hours we sat, listening to occult teachings. The awkwardness of the situation was in that the parents spoke not a single word of English, but they politely smiled and nodded over Karma, reincarnation, the tilting of the Earth's axis. Despite repeated attempts on our part to change the conversation, the other two held firmly for the evening.

What was gained? Where these people ready for this exposure? Hardly. The two people, regardless of years of study, missed one of the basic principles—the Law of Attraction. In time, as you study more, apply more, and reflect more, those who are ready will come to you.

Never, never impose your knowledge and experiences upon others. Wait to be asked. And when asked, how far do you go? Here, apply the Law of Discrimination, for you must never give more than what the person is ready for, and never give advice. Listen and explain the workings of the Laws, cite your own experiences, but always permit them to decide that action to follow. You will have the urge or the tendency to step in, but people must have the privilege of learning themselves. By solving problems for others, you rob them of the necessary growing experiences. Even if they make the wrong decision, they will, eventually, grow out of that. It is, often, not easy to sit on the sidelines and watch friends and relatives and neighbors make mistakes. The closer you are, the more trying the situation can become. However, remember that each must solve his own problems.'

If you offer a solution from the light of your own knowledge or experiences or if you solve the problem, it could result in disaster. In the event that things do not go well, you will find that people will project blame and guilt upon you.

Remember that you cannot be all things to all men. Also, by becoming involved in the problems of others, you neglect your own evolvement and your own Karma. Always help those in need but do not step in where you should not. Use the Law of Discretion.

All of this depends upon you, for the decision must be yours and yours alone. Eventually, all who attain to Truth must return in service to others. Only through compassionate service can Mastership and Illumination be reached.

It sounds rather lonely, yet when you reach this point, you are never alone. All forces of the Cosmic unite to assist, and the Ascended Masters guide you along the way. You become, in reality, a conscious Cosmic Unit (Atom), directing your worldly activity consciously. The At-one-ment brings the realization that all men are your brothers; their problems are yours; their successes and failures are your successes and failures.

It only appears to be an exhausting work. Yet, when you are at this point, you will have the energy and the health, the work, the abilities, facilities, and opportunities to accomplish it all. The Cosmic is well aware of what is required and what you need. The supply is unlimited and is available actually, to all. Recall the words, "When one reaches up, all is given him. Seek ye first the Kingdom of Heaven and all else shall be added." You find that you possess the key to the answers of all of life and of all things in that life. You will remain a part—a compassionate part of life—yet are detached from the impingements of the material world. The Cosmic music, or Music of the Spheres, is yours to hear at all times, at all places, and in everything. All experiences of life assume the identical character—that of Divine Love and Harmony.

To achieve this, you must accept life with its problems and apply yourself until through the very effort made, you scale the heights to spiritual unfoldment and Divine Light. Only by so doing can you arrive here. There is no other way than by sacrifice and endeavor. It must be remembered that upon reaching the goal, all Cosmic Power comes, accompanied by worldly opportunities which grant you the ability to cope with and to manage the externalized world. Most people stop at world reality, not being able to conceive or to continuously strive for the "Pearl of Great Wisdom."

All of evolution is spiral, and soul consciousness assumes the identical spiral form. Truth, like matter, is always "becoming," and as you reach an "apparent" final stage of evolvement to Truth, you discover that you must penetrate deeper than ever into the creative mysteries. The Ring-Pass-Not is flexible and ever expanding—as is the Universe, as is the Cosmos.

Still, it is will and desire which will determine how far you will penetrate the mysteries. This stage is the stage of the Adepts, and even they sometimes fail, for they go it alone. Adepts must, at this level, renounce the possessions of the material world, exhibit detachment for the externalized (physical) expression of the Word made manifest. Here, too, the Adept has a choice, for he can go on to higher spiritual planes or contribute his awareness and knowledge in service to the rest of humanity and all members of all kingdoms.

Humanity itself and the learning processes of humanity give the fabric from which you form the highest initiation. As you consciously experience life and endeavor to transmute the lower self, you add material to the framework for adepthood. All experience, however, is the important factor, not just the major one or ones. No matter how small the experience, it contributes understanding of life in its varied phases and will present the key to the door of wisdom. Once attained, it is never lost despite the fact that the Adept, too, might lose his way a bit because of failure in determination or lack of attention to the disciplines of the Laws. You yourself are the symbol of the key—through the demonstration of your higher, Divine self.

Difficult though it might seem, the stability and surety of attainment, even at this level, will largely depend upon how much has been learned, how much of the Laws has been applied, how much you have experienced. The resultant structure of the Adept reminds you of the "house built on sand and those built on rock." It is far better to grow slowly (all growth is slow, actually) but surely and obey the Cosmic principles so that when you reach the level of spiritual Truth, you can unlock the door by yourself and step forward to even greater heights of spiritual evolvement. At the crossing of the threshold of the doorway, you stand alone with your Soul and the Cosmic.

Here you become one with the Divine Center, the Universal Mind—all that has been, is, and ever will be, for all is ONE. All is in all. You express spirituality working through the points of the six-pointed star, the dual principle of the triangle or Trinity. Too, you now function on a higher plane of consciousness, impervious to earthly negativism. It is on the higher planes, the fourth dimension and higher, that the White Brotherhoods from the positive polarity center their forces and send forth the Cosmic Laws to the material world. These White Brotherhoods receive the Cosmic Laws through the one known as the Golden Pheasant which receives its directions from the Ascended Masters. Now, by working through and with these higher spiritual forces, you, the Initiate, know that "I and the Father are one." You contribute your developed force and becoming a working partner with the Ultimate. Whatever was sacrificed in order to attain to this stage of evolvement is given back—and more, for the "bread was cast upon the waters," but now you realize the proper place of all things and use everything in service. This stage of "be-ness' comples you to walk among your fellow man, doing your Father's work, and while thus engaged, you have the force, knowledge, and methods to achieve all. In all of this, the Cosmic protection surrounds you. Wherever you go, the influence of your higher self, emanating through your auric field, influences people and the manifested members of the lower kingdoms. Knowing the oneness that pervades the universe knowing that all is in all, knowing that within the grain of sand is the universe, walk in the midst of adversity and sorrow, in the midst of prosperity and joy, and see it all as one manifestation of the ALL.

An adept, too has choices, and he can either work among the

kingdoms or ascend with higher degrees of being. There is what is known as the THIRD DEGREE, one of the highest divisions of the White Brotherhood. Once on the THIRD DEGREE, the material limitations are transcended—all is one in completeness. No longer is the adept subject to the physical senses and the pains derived therefrom. He can peruse the Akashic Records—every page—know all that there is to be known, is one with each unit of creation, and can function through and with all of nature.

Everything rests with you, your motives, the desires behind these motives, the efforts you put forth to attain full spiritual unfoldment. The WAY is open to you if you would but try, learn, and apply the Cosmic Law while experiencing life. The key to the door is service to all facets of the manifested creation through the evolved and awakened psychic centers within you.

THE DEVELOPMENT
OF PSYCHIC POWERS

The human mind is something like a current in a river; the river a collective flow of many currents.
To attempt to give a patent formula for development of psychic powers suggests that by following certain steps in thinking processes and meditation exercises, you may remove your current from the river.
Not likely!
In this chapter, the author sketches a few contours of some meditation practices and they are no more than the first faltering steps in a path of development that is studded with stumbling blocks and diversions. This should be clear at the outset; there is no giant step to self-development. No drugs, no hypnotist and no teacher can give an aspirant a magic potion or suggestion that will result in "instant illumination".
If anything in this chapter implies otherwise, you have misread it. Steer clear of the promise of fast routes to developing psychic power. They're more likely to be fast routes to a dead end at best and self deterioration or destruction at worst.

It is a confused world in which you find yourselves confused—politically, ethnically, economically, and religiously. No area in the institutions of man escapes the rampant chaos of the present age. So, it is no wonder that people are looking for "something" that will present a form of recourse from the upset and disturbances. Since the old establishments are involved in this situation and, apparently, no longer suffice for personal satisfaction, people are turning to other or are re-discovering discarded schools of thought and activity from the past.

Today, it seems that people want some sort of personal "island" of their own to which they can retreat, find peace of mind, stability in an unstable world, and yet remain a part of the physical realm into which they were born.

Metaphysics, as stated previously, does offer this retreat—a personal, gratifying retreat which grants you relief (through understanding), yet emphasizes the importance of involvement in the plane of physical, dense matter.

How do you, as a person, find this haven for yourself. Stop looking for an imaginary place, a Shangri-La, isolated from the work-a-day environment. It is no further away than you are, for you are the haven, the island you seek. It is all within yourself, and you but have to insert the key to unlock or unleash the dormant powers and potentials that reside within. Christ said, "Go to the temple within." *You* are the Temple and the New Jerusalem.

This fervent search, especially among the young people, expresses itself today in becoming "followers" of self-styled Gurus, seers, groups that advertise that they guarantee the development of your inner powers so that you might rise from the dank and muddy soil of today's experiences. How often have you noticed the ads in periodicals which promise a sort of capsule version of psychic development—in six easy lessons, so to speak?

Never before in the long history of man's search for Truth has he come so close nor so sincerely has desired the Truth. It is the Aquarian Age with the water bearer which symbolizes man's progress into the spirituality of life that stimulates humanity to the reawakening of the God qualities within. For you *are* Gods-in-the-making. Christ said, "Even as I have done, so can ye also, and more."

Everyone of you should read Cole's GODS IN THE MAKING, one of the finest books to develop the theme of evolving soul through all of the kingdoms and species.

Since you, as a member of the race and the life stream of the planet, have reached a crisis as a planetary life-atom, the Cosmic has stepped up the evolutionary rate so that you might avail yourselves of the greater opportunities for expression of the Higher or Divine Self. The time is NOW!

Unfortunately, as evidenced by the course of history, every great period brings negative qualities to the fore as well as the positive. Since all of life rests on the principle of duality (read Plato), this is understandable. It is regretable that most of mankind accepts negativity as it is so misconstrued—an evil force—rather than viewing negative as the energy force, the obstacles that test us all and grant the opportunities to transmute to the higher degree of the positive activity.

So it is in the present time that each of you is searching for your own "island", striving to express spiritual reality in a world steeped in misused materialism. With this common emphasis on self-development have come groups and schools which latch on the the current "band-wagon" and offer hopes and rewards in soul-searching experiences, illumination, psychic development.

Many who lack contact with groups such as these above-mentioned, resort to artifical means to develop psychic powers. The use of drugs to open the centers, indiscriminately, will result in disaster. The very goal sought by the drug users is destroyed by this method. Initial involvement with drugs indicates the promise of unusual experiences, at first, but the metaphysically unschooled person does not know that the use of drugs results in the burning out of the psychic centers.

When this happens, it requires many incarnations before the opportunities are presented to you again. What a person is really doing, when using drugs, is committing spiritual suicide.

So, where does all this then leave you in the picture of your probing for spiritual stability? Where do you look for the answer? What are the approved methods you might try to achieve what you desire yet avoid the pitfalls which are so prevalent in this area?

First, you must still follow the Cosmic Laws of Acceptance, Attention, and, Attraction. Accept the fact that "You are where you are meant to be." Perhaps psychic development is not your particular baliwick anyway. Spirituality can still be yours without the phenomenal aspects of psychism. Maybe your attention should be on "the job at hand", the "Eternal Now", where you are, doing the best you can with what you have. By so doing, you might just experience being "the last which shall come first." Realize that when you are ready, the teacher appears, and by the Law of Attraction, all that you have earned and *can handle* will come your way.

Forcing the issue can be detrimental to your steady progress, and it is a steady progress as you study, learn, and apply the Cosmic Laws in work, sacrifice, and service to others. Do not expect great and exhilerating psychic experiences as evidence of spiritual evolvement, but rather "enter into the kingdom as little children"—with humility without humbleness, pride without being proud. "Seek the kingdom within" should be your guide post.

For those of you who still wish to utilize developmental methods, there are systems which have been carefully devised to guide you in this endeavor. Again, use great caution, guard your motives and the desires behind these motives. *It can* all be yours if you so wish it.

METHODS OF DEVELOPING PSYCHIC POWERS

There are many methods advocated in which you can develop your psychic powers. The ones most generally suggested in metaphysical circles are:

1. The Oriental Method: If you wish to follow this avenue, you must be prepared to devote many years of study and to spend hours at practice. This approach involves breath control and voice training (sound is important), a diet which must be strictly adhered to, physical training dealing with assorted positions and fitness development, emphasis on physical and mental disciplines, and periods of complete retreat from the problems of the world. This method naturally, finds many followers in the Eastern cultures of Tibet, China, India.

2. The Artificial Stimulant Method: Similar to the indiscriminate use of LSD and trance producing mushrooms of Mexico, this method employs chemicals, herbs, etc. as means to increase psychic powers. The problem encountered here is that addiction could result. Another effect could be the reverse of desired goals, for although temporarily presenting glimpses of the Ultimate, the stimulants bring disaster in the form of burning out the psychic centers so that no psychic development takes place. Many incarnations are then needed before you again reach the stage in which you are ready to develop these potentials.

3. The Mesmeric Method: This method falls back on what is termed "animal magnetism"—a physical exchange which takes place between the one who is trying to magnetize and the person attempting to develop his psychic powers. Here you, as the developing sensitive, receive a subtle fluid from the body of the "magnetizer". This is accomplished in what are commonly known as "passes". In Christian Science circles this "animal magnetism" is often referred to and recognized. One danger here to both the magnetizer and the

sensitive is that of depletion of energy, resulting in fatigue, which automatically prevents proper development and, often, subjects both to environmental influences and illnesses.

4. The Hypnotic Method: By employing the usual hypnotic mechanisms, the sensitive is placed in a trance and subject to mental suggestion. This implies control by one and subjection by the other. One will become superimposed upon another, an action directly opposed to the Law which states that each person must, at all times, be in complete command of all his faculties. Hypnotism does not bring *real* development but rather *imposed* or dictated development. No sensitive retains or uses properly what has been encouraged through the Hypnotic Method. Growth and development necessitate full awareness of all faculties. Hypnotism is but a phenomena aspect of metaphysics and should always be relegated to this function only.

5. The Cooperative Method: Among the true metaphysicians, this method has been considered the most practical and scientific for those who desire psychic sensitivity. The approach is reasonable and results more definite and longer lasting.

There are many advantages to the Co-operative method. Primarily, its strength lies in the fact that is rooted in the known laws of the psychic world. Knowledge of the laws should be the first step any sensitive takes to developing psychic powers. Too, the Co-operative Method suits the Western culture and living more so than the Oriental Method, which would be most impractical in the West. There is no need for any sort of equipment—just the sensitive is all that is required. In the Co-operative method, a person could work alone, not requiring the services of advanced or developed mediums. Another favorable aspect is that there are no ill effects produced upon the person using the method. Time devoted depends upon the individual and, in actuality, demands little in time and effort.

Let us examine more fully this method and its guide lines for developing psychic forces.

Basically, of course, the sensitive must entertain the belief that there are other planes of existence, other beings to whom you can turn for aid in developing yourself. Proof of the continuity of life and consciousness can be found in all religions (miracles) and in many case histories of individual experiences. The other planes of life and the other beings are on call for all who reach up to them.

Those above help those below. A caution is necessary here, for there are the mischief makers, undeveloped entities, and negative forces, especially on the Astral Plane, and you must guard against their influences. In the steps listed, this will be shown to you.

Definite procedures should be followed when first you attempt to develop yourself psychically. The procedures represent a form of discipline—necessary, initially, but dispensed with once the development is assured. Then, all is as natural as breathing.

You hear much about Meditation. It *is* extremely important, but so much has been written about it; so many have so much to say about how to go into meditation, what you should see during this experience, what it all means.

Meditation is the foundation for all psychic enhancement, but its success or failure rests entirely with the individual. Since all experience, all knowledge, all proof is individual, so is meditation a matter of individual preference and procedure. What might suit one and bring results might not be a compatible method for another. Schools of thought on meditation should only be guides to methods and possible procedures, in a general sense. They should *never* be definite ways for any *one* person.

The purpose of meditation should be to relax you, to eliminate the impingements of the external world, to establish a rapport between you and the Higher Forces. This is not easy to accomplish, for few of you know how to relax. You are too tense, wound up from the affairs of your daily life. Try this to relax; it might work for you.

Find a quiet spot, comfortable, and easy, but without a clutter of items around you that might attract your attention. Close your eyes softly. Try to *sense* the muscles of the face falling easily into a relaxed state—almost a collapsing sort of feeling. When and if this is done, you can move on to the rest of the body and, eventually, relax it all.

During all of this, your attention is on your body and you do not react or are aware of outside noises or environmental factors.

Now, you are relaxed, but how do you prevent your thoughts from wandering back to the incidents of the day? How about the nagging problems in your life? Time and time again, you drift back into these thoughts, catch yourself, and attempt again to meditate.

But, what are you meditating on which will transport your thoughts from the aggravating daily experiences? Some claim you fix your attention on an idea, wallow in it, pursue it through all corridors of your mind. Others feel that this is what you are attempting to avoid and that it limits meditative results. Yogic groups center attention on the forehead between the eyes, for here is located the "third eye" or psychic center. With the eyes closed, you fix your eyes as if they are looking at this spot. This can cause some strain for you.

Another method is to sit quietly, eliminate all thoughts, and let come what may. This, too, can be a sort of drifting.

Each of you must find his own particular method, for no one method suits all. Whatever is comfortable for you, whatever brings results *is* your own special technique.

I find the greatest result by lying down (a method frowned upon by metaphysical groups, for the spine must be upright). For me, it works, and that is all I can ask and all you can ask of the system you use.

Time is always stressed for meditation periods, and the usual statement made is to have an established, daily routine. If you meditate at 6:00 p.m. one day, do it at the same time every day. However, again, can a routine be adhered to faithfully? Is your life so rigidly fixed that you *know* that at 6:00 p.m. you will be free everyday? To me, the matter of exactness in time is for disciplinary purposes, but not necessary. Perhaps it is far wiser for you to meditate (daily) when you are quiet, when there are no others around to interfere, or when you are "in the mood", so to speak.

What really matters is that you take time out of your busy day to meditate. Even if nothing comes to you, you have relaxed, elevated your desires, and can return refreshed to your chores.

How long should the meditation period be? The usual length is from ten to twenty or twenty-five minutes, twenty-five minutes being rather long actually. Again, who can definitely set limits for someone else? Each of you must find his own time limit. As your sensitivity increases, you will achieve more in a shorter time.

Various meditation groups and schools advocate that the position of the hands, head, legs, etc. are all important. Perhaps this should be observed, in the beginning, but does not necessarily hold true later on. Also, you could bog yourself down with all these little ritualistic requirements. It all should be just comfortable, quiet, practical, and very simple—nothing more than that.

Too, lighting in the room should be regulated to eliminate glaring light; dimness, but not darkness is preferred. Total darkness is to be avoided in the early stages of meditation experiences. Also, emphasis has been placed on using the same location for meditation; this is for two reasons: First, you know how a familiar environment causes you to feel "at home". Every time that you change the meditation area, you have to adjust to the entire atmosphere of where you now are. Secondly, in using the same place, you build into it a vibration which assists you in succeeding meditative attempts. Gradually, a vortex of power accumulates for you in that spot.

The room temperature must be conducive to comfort—not too warm or too cold—and drafts should be provided against.

Prior to all of this, there must have been certain measures taken by you in preparation for a meditation period. Personal cleanliness is necessary. Imagine coming into a meditation directly after weeding in a garden, painting doors, exercising. Your body is soiled and perspiration is present. How could you be comfortable?

Wearing apparel should not be tight or confining in any manner. A tight belt or tie can cause discomfort.

I found that lecturing and meditations were easier if I had not consumed a great deal of food beforehand. No stimulants should have been resorted to for several hours previous to the meditative period, but especially drugs and alcohol should be avoided.

Your attitudes could prevent any meditation period from being successful. Are you going into meditation because of upsetting conditions in the family? Are you overly concerned with finances, illness, or any problems? Do you feel insecure at work, in social affairs? Are these on your mind before a meditation period? Are these the reasons for meditation?

Meditation is to attune yourself with Higher Forces, to evolve spiritually. Basically, this is it. Side results might solve your worries, bring good health, and indicate solutions to situations. Primarily though, the purpose is to increase sensitivity, to become at-one with the Cosmic. Anyone who has studied metaphysics *knows* that this is true meditation, and when you do meditate correctly, all areas of your life improve.

Be sure that your goal is the Higher Planes. Put out the thought before meditating that you will reach above the Astral Plane and not be trapped in the morass of undeveloped forces which inhabit the Astral realms. This is the area which most mediums become involved with. It is a rare medium, indeed, who manages to reach even the upper strata of the Astral.

So, enter meditation periods with proper attitudes and with constructive thoughts and desires.

Where do you now find yourself regarding meditation? All is prepared—the physical surroundings and your personal preparations. What now?

Advocates of the Co-operative Method stress a course of action for the Meditation Period which could be rather exacting in its demands and contains a flavor of ritualism. They contend that it is a scientific program, and in reviewing their program, it seems to be based on ancient Tibetan principles dealing with mantric sounds and symbols, and these find their foundations in scientifically proved theories.

Unfortunately, through the many centuries of passing on the Truths, much has fallen into *disuse* and *abuse* and often utilized without *knowing* the real principles involved. Concentration revolves around the *act* rather than the *purpose* and so loses much strength and power. It is, also, very fortunate that the mantric symbols and sounds, in themselves, are harmless when used by those ignorant of the inherent power. It has no effect at that time. However, remember the Principle of Duality and Polarity, for, in the wrong hands, these same symbols and sounds can be encouraged for the negative as well as for the positive. The Black Brotherhood exists as well as the White Brotherhood.

Do not become alarmed at this reference to the Brotherhoods. So many become alarmed by the words, "Black Brotherhood", "evil", "Satan", etc. In reality, they represent *not* evil, for there is no such thing, but rather the *misuse* of good. Therefore, we can safely say that there is no evil—just good misused.

So let us return to the course of action prescribed to by those who have a program for entering into the Meditation Period.

First the Invocation. This, supposedly, puts you in open rapport with the Higher Forces and (some claim) the Ascended Masters. It is meant to be an invitation to assist you in your endeavor to offer yourself as a channel through which these developed Entities can function.

To me, it is interesting to note that the Co-operative Method followers do state that the Invocation can be uttered aloud or can be stated silently. Many groups insist on verbal invocation—to build up force fields of energy. Frankly, the silent Invocation has as much to offer (if not more) in strength as the oral one. In many ways, and here I stand firmly despite attacks which might be directed at me, the oral Invocation indicates less developed sensitives and less knowledgeable leaders.

You have all heard dissertation on the power of "silent prayer" and "thought" and the forms which can be created through them. Also, an idea or thought can be much weakened by being "talked out"—all of the energy dissipating itself in the loud assertions of the thought. The genius thinks his way, silently and carefully, and produces something. It is always "his", in a sense. Invocations, prayers, thoughts, (call them what you will) are always "yours" in silence and stronger because of this.

Besides recommending an Invocation, some groups require a definite, established word-for-word type. Again, this is not necessary, for an established Invocation serves only as a guide for you—should you wish to employ it.

What Invocation do you wish to use? What words should be stated or included? Frankly, just be yourself. You have a goal—to evolve spiritually and to develop your psychic powers. Why not address this very thought to the Cosmic Forces? They can detect your sincerity of purpose, your degree of effort, your level of evolvement and your need.

So, let it rest at that. However, *you* decide—Invocation (oral or silent) or thought (established or spontaneous). By your sincerity, effort, and need results will be evidenced regardless of techniques resorted to.

Most of you pass through each day little realizing the psychic powers you possess and, thus, never use them. So these forces lie dormant within you, and the purpose of sensitizing yourself through meditation is to energize these powers to make them operate twenty-four hours a day in all aspects of your life. The Meditation Period and the Invocation are the opening wedges or keys to open the door of your "inner self." The "inner self", once awakened, then manifests through the material, physical body in the mundane affairs of life.

Once the psychic centers are aroused, you become aware of *all* the psychic forces that constantly surround you and are available to be utilized. All the Higher Forces' powers exist for you to contact when you are ready.

The question now arises: How do you open the door to psychic powers? This is the second step of the Co-operative Method, and it requires the use of Affirmations, which are positive statements used to "set the stage." Mrs. Mady Badkin, a wonderfully evolved soul, everyday said, "I'm alive, alert, awake, and enthusiastic." This she said three times and even applied a tune to it. She meant it all, and it served as a guide for her during the day. It set the tone of her day for her, and others reacted to her vibrations, for her vibrations were effective.

What are you doing is applying Cosmic Energy in Affirmations. They work; they are effective; they are available for you to use. Again, your choice enters into the picture as to whether or not the use of affirmations is your province in programming yourself for meditations.

Many of you might resent using Affirmations, basing opposition on the grounds of ritualistic encroachment. If you feel this way, do not use set statements. Think of your psychic centers being awakened, a force-field of energy surging within you. Feel this and it will be so, and it will carry the same weight as any Affirmation.

The Co-operative Method's third step invokes a protection for you—the Law of Protection. Each of you must qualify the unleashing of the influence within you. Remember that once you cross the threshold of psychic development, you become susceptible to both aspects of the polarity. You, certainly, do not wish to be effected by *all* sorts and *all* levels of psychic forces or phenomena. Divers psychic agencies exist, ready to exert their strength upon every and any of you who embark on this endeavor. Not all of them could you handle unless you have been properly schooled in Truth to discriminate what to accept and what to reject.

Again, the Co-operative Method supports the use of Affirmations regarding the Law of Protection—known as a "Protective Affirmation." The supporters of the Co-operative Method feel that it is a mental command or rejection of designated types of psychic forces. This could be highly questioned, for many a developed psychic has been fooled by a negative entity which clothed itself in the costume of Higher Thought.

The greatest protection you can have, even in this segment of metaphysics, is your skepticism. Be skeptical, but keep an open mind and seek proof. Build a sound body of knowledge for yourself so that as you become *involved* in the *evolvement*, your knowledge acts as a protection as well. Sincerity, effort, desire and the motives behind the desire serve you in attracting the best to you—according to the level of your own development.

Remember the attitudes with which you entered into the Meditation Period. These represent the Law of Protection as surely as any Affirmation for protection. By the Law of Attraction, you bring to yourself that which you earn by virtue of your attitudes and purposes in attempting meditation. Deeply rooted in the recesses of your subconscious mind are the real and definite attitudes, regardless of what you might affirm verbally.

So, Affirmations do serve if you need them, feel comfortable, and are very sincere. Thought, attitudes, sincerity of effort equally contribute to protecting you from negative influences.

Before passing on to the next step, I should like to relate an incident that occurred to someone I once knew. A man, let's call him Mr. J., decided to delve deeply into the development of psychic forces within him. His intention was to reach into the higher planes beyond those that man is permitted to enter. He had a smattering of occult knowledge, but, apparently, either not enough in quantity or quality or not enough understanding. His methods were abrupt and forceful, for he was determined to accomplish this. The net result of his experience was a stroke and a "possession" that took place. Mr. J. was confined to a wheel chair for almost two years and had a speech impediment added to his problem.

After two years, he was brought to a highly developed individual who worked with this man for about three hours. At the end of the three hours, the possession was gone—an exorcism had been performed. He walked as normally as he had before the incident, and his speech was restored to a normal condition. He had "rushed in where angles fear to tread" and so suffered the consequences. If I recall, he learned quite a lesson and proceeded more cautiously and obtained finer and greater results. He did not attempt to reach into the higher planes.

Armed with knowledge and skepticism, should you be subjected to negative forces, stop the meditation period. Something, somewhere is not operating correctly. Re-check all the previous stops. If all is in order, then your basic attitudes and sincerity of purpose could be hindering accomplishment.

About ten years ago, I was invited by a couple to witness the psychic phenomena of clairvoyance and the other areas of the psychic world which the lady had been experiencing. We talked a while, and then the scene was set. I became slightly astonished to observe the physical preparations. The husband brought in a chaise lounge, covered it with several blankets, shut all doors and windows. The lady stretched out on the lounge, and her husband proceeded to envelop her in the blankets. Only her head and arms were free. Lights were put out completely; her husband and I sat on either side, each one of us holding the corresponding hand.

Well, what ensued rather startled me. Screams, groans, moans issued from the throat of the lady. Her entire body shook; her legs, encased in the blanket, thrashed on the lounge. The darkness was black enough, but some other force—all I can describe it by is "a black-blackness—seemed to encompass us all.

Fortunately, I had studied enough and had been trained properly so that I could ward off this "force" which disturbed me. I spend the next half hour fighting to maintain balance and to prevent the "blackness" from taking over.

When the demonstration was over and a slight conversation held, I excused myself from their presence and from that house. I have never gone back since.

Why did this occur? In reviewing the discussion previous to the actual event, it became clear that all psychic development, any technique or knowledge learned would be used by them for personal gain—money-making, in particular. The attitudes and purposes were wrong and so, the result was negative. I count my blessings in that I was not affected by any of it.

The next step in the Meditation Period is known as the State of Passivity. It is a state in which your body is completely relaxed and the mind is stilled. Only when this state exists can you attune yourself psychically to the Higher Forces and Higher Planes. This is all a result of the preparations mentioned before. Those who subscribe to the Co-operative Method feel that this state is a prerequisite to psychic attunement.

The Co-operative Method then stipulates that once the rapport has been established between you, the Higher Forces, and Planes, it is necessary to maintain this rapport. There are three types that you can pursue which are to regulate and develop your sensitivity.

1. Psychic Sensitization Work in which you manipulate the psychic and nervous energies.
2. Experimental Work in which the Higher Forces determine the psychic power development which you have attained to,
3. Production Work in which the Higher Forces actually exercise your psychic powers and, by so doing, increase the development.

In these steps, caution must be exercised, for you must *know* definitely that it is the Higher Forces stimulating or increasing your psychic powers. By employing the Law of Protection, you can ward off any negative entities which might attempt to use you as a channel for their work.

Now that you have everything defined, procedures are established, you should be ready to receive meditative impressions or results.

What will you see and what will it all mean? There can be as many psychic impressions and as many interpretations as there are those who delve into this activity. Experiences can range from just colors, geometric figures, to actual images or scenes. Some metaphysicians place great store in color; some, in geometric patterns. What do you believe and whom do you believe?

Belief rests solely upon proof—individual proof—and not with someone outside of the experience itself. Qualities have been ascribed to colors by every metaphysical group since the beginning of time, and, on these, you could be fairly sure in interpretation.

Geometric patterns assume as many meanings as modern art—all in the eye of the beholder. Images fall into this classification as well. *No one* can really interpret your meditation impressions any more than anyone can interpret dreams. Oh, to be sure, there will always be those who will claim to be able to do so, to give life-readings of past lives, to read the Akashic Records. However, in the long run, you are the *only* one who will really know.

ABOUT THE AUTHOR

A student of occult sciences for 45 years, Mr. Yott now spends his time writing and lecturing in astrology and metaphysics. Mr. Yott graduated from Drew University and continued his studies at William Patterson College, Montclair State College, Rutgers University, Mexico City College and the University of Valencia in Spain. A retired high school teacher and former librarian, he is the founder of the North Jersey Metaphysical Center and has taught occult subjects in adult education programs since 1956.

Photo by Charles Moretz

* * *

Astrology and Reincarnation Volume 1
RETROGRADE PLANETS AND REINCARNATION

Volume 1 of this series provides a thorough explanation of the retrograde condition of each planet through the twelve houses of the zodiac, suggesting the ways in which an individual may transmute the negative energy inherent in the retrograde in order to grow and evolve in this lifetime.

Astrology and Reincarnation Volume 2
INTERCEPTED SIGNS AND REINCARNATION

Volume 2 examines each intercepted sign and its opposite as they appear through the houses of the zodiac, pointing out the areas in which we failed to develop and grow in past lifetimes, and showing how we may transmute our past weaknesses into present strengths.

Astrology and Reincarnation Volume 3
TRIANGULATION OF SATURN-JUPITER-MERCURY

In order to interpret the effects of reincarnation in a chart, the astrologer must look to where Saturn, Jupiter and Mercury are located. Saturn represents the sum total of a native's Karma; Jupiter demonstrates the area in which one may best work out one's Karma; and Mercury instructs the individual in *how* he can best work out his Karma. This last volume of the *Astrology and Reincarnation Series* takes Saturn through the twelve houses of the zodiac. In a free-flowing association, Mr. Yott discusses the triangulation of Jupiter and Mercury to Saturn in each of the houses, describing the metaphysical purpose of this particular incarnation and mapping out the means by which we may experience, develop and grow into more perfect human beings.

* * *

by
Donald H. Yott

A SELECTION OF OUR ASTROLOGY TITLES:

SATURN: A NEW LOOK AT AN OLD DEVIL, Liz Greene. Tracing the character of this most important planet through sign, house, aspect and synastry, and its role in mythology, Dr. Greene provides a brilliant analysis which sheds light on that mysterious, elusive entity that psychology calls the self. Paper

RELATING: AN ASTROLOGICAL GUIDE TO LIVING WITH OTHERS ON A SMALL PLANET, Liz Greene. Dr. Greene uses basic astrological concepts symbolically and practically, in a framework of Jungian psychology, to show the ways in which people relate to one another on both conscious and unconscious levels. An original, advanced, information-packed, provocative and well-organized work. Cloth

THE COMPOSITE CHART, John Townley. This is a new technique in the ancient art of horoscope comparison. It is useful as a fundamental astrological technique such as solar and lunar returns and horary charts. Paper

ASTROLOGICAL CYCLES AND THE LIFE CRISIS PERIODS, John Townley. This book explores the repeating cycles manifested in man and nature, from full-moon lunacy to social upheaval. Special emphasis on the psychological personality-crisis periods—when they occur and how people deal with them. Paper

FIRST STEPS TO ASTROLOGY, Preston Crowmarsh. *Paths to Inner Power Series.* Gives practical groundwork essential to a proper understanding of Astrology. Paper

JUPITER, Alan Leo. Jupiter presented as the Presever, with an analysis of its remarkable symbolism. Paper

ENCYCLOPEDIA OF MEDICAL ASTROLOGY, Dr. H.L. Cornell. An alphabetical listing of medical conditions, areas of the body, and specific diseases with planetary aspects listed which affect them. Cloth

THE ASTROLOGY OF I CHING, W.K. Chu & W.A. Sherrill. This first English translation of an ancient manuscript unfolds the use of *I Ching* in Astrology. In this system, one calculates the state of the heavenly and earthly forces for the date, time and place of one's birth thus arriving at a natal hexagram. THE ASTROLOGY OF I CHING can be a yearly, monthly and daily guide for spiritual development, furthering our understanding of heaven and earth and harmonizing life with the ways of nature.

THE PRENATAL EPOCH, E.H. Bailey. Rectification of recorded birth times and the calculation of the time of birth from past events with reference to and check by Epocal Laws. Cloth

THE NEW WAITE'S COMPENDIUM OF NATAL ASTROLOGY, Colin Evans. With Ephemeris for 1870-1980 and Universal Table of Houses, Cloth

PLUTO-NEPTUNE, Germaine Holley. This book on the Pluto-Neptune dual rulership of Pisces goes beyond an analysis of psychological conditioning, opening the gate to a new philosophical perspective. Paper

TRANSCENDENTAL ASTROLOGY, A.G.S. Norris. The planetary numerals and symbolism, and the lessons of the signs, delineated allowing the astrologer to link the soul to the astrological chart. Cloth

BEGINNERS GUIDE TO PRACTICAL ASTROLOGY, Vivian Robson. An introductory book on astrology containing all the information needed for a practical investigation of astrological claims. Paper

ELECTIONAL ASTROLOGY, Vivian Robson. The choosing, or electing, of propitious times for the commencement of any undertaking. Cloth

THE FIXED STARS AND CONSTELLATIONS IN ASTROLOGY, Vivian Robson. Contains much of what has been written on this subject since the Middle Ages. Cloth

THE ZODIAC AND THE SALTS OF SALVATION, Inez Eudora Perry & George Washington Carey. The relation of the mineral salts of the body to the Signs of the Zodiac and an esoteric analysis and synthesis of the Zodiacal Signs and their physical-chemical allocations. Cloth

YOUR CHARACTER FROM THE STARS, T. Mawbry Cole. *Path to Inner Power Series* Introductory analysis of character and physical characteristics of the signs of the Zodiac. Paper